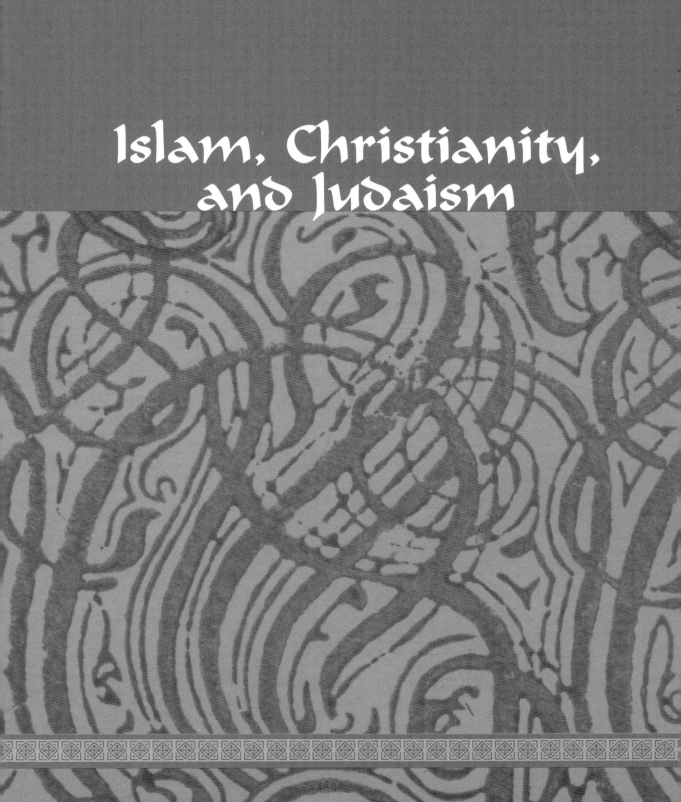

Islam, Christianity, and Judaism

Introducing Islam

Islam, Christianity, and Judaism

Dorothy Kavanaugh

Produced by OTTN Publishing, Stockton, New Jersey

Mason Crest Publishers
370 Reed Road
Broomall, PA 19008
www.masoncrest.com

3 5 7 9 8 6 4 2

Library of Congress Cataloging-in-Publication Data

Kavanaugh, Dorothy, 1969-
  Islam, Christianity, Judaism / Dorothy Kavanaugh.
      p. cm. — (Introducing Islam)
  Includes bibliographical references and index.
  ISBN 1-59084-698-2
  1. Judaism—Juvenile literature. 2. Christianity—Juvenile literature.
  3. Islam—Juvenile literature. I. Title. II. Series.
  BM573.K35 2004
  201'.5—dc22
                              2004005635

Contents

Introduction

The central belief of Islam, one of the world's major religions, is contained in a simple but powerful phrase: "There is no god but Allah, and Muhammad is His prophet." The Islamic faith, which emerged from the Arabian desert in the seventh century C.E., has become one of the world's most important and influential religions.

Within a century after the death of the Prophet Muhammad, Islam had spread throughout the Arabian Peninsula into Europe, Africa, and Asia. Today, Muslims can be found throughout the globe, and Islam is the world's fastest-growing religion. There are about 1.25 billion Muslims, which means that approximately one of every five people follows Islam. The global total of believers has surpassed two older religions, Hinduism and Buddhism; only Christianity has more followers.

Muslims can also be found in North America. Many Muslims have immigrated to the United States and Canada, and large numbers of people—particularly African Americans—have converted to Islam since the 1960s. Today, there are an estimated 6 million Muslims in the United States, with an additional half-million Muslims in Canada.

Despite this growing popularity, many people in the West are uninformed about Islam. For many Americans, their only exposure to this important religion, with its glorious history and rich culture, is through news reports about wars in Muslim countries, terrorist attacks, or fundamentalist denunciations of Western corruption.

The purpose of the INTRODUCING ISLAM series is to provide an objective examination of Islam and give an overview of what Muslims believe, how they practice their faith, and what values they hold most important. Four volumes in particular focus on Islamic beliefs and religious practices. *Islam: The Basics* answers the essential questions about the faith and provides information about the major sects. *Islam, Christianity, and Judaism* describes and explains the similarities and differences between these three great monotheistic religions. *Heroes and Holy Places* gives information about such important figures as Muhammad and Saladin, as well as shrines like Mecca and Jerusalem. *Islamic Fundamentalism* focuses on the emergence of the Islamist movement during the 20th century, the development of an Islamist government in Iran, and the differences between Islamists and moderates in such countries as Algeria, Indonesia, and Egypt.

Two volumes in the series explore Islam in the United States, and the relationship between the Muslim world and the West. *The American Encounter with Islam* provides specific history about Muslims in North America from the 17th century until the present, and traces the development of uniquely American sects like the Nation of Islam. *Muslims and the West* attempts to put the encounter between two important civilizations in broader perspective from a historical point of view.

Recent statistical data is extensively provided in two volumes, in order to discuss life in the Muslim world. *Who Are the Muslims?* is a geopolitical survey that explores the many different cultures that can be found in the Muslim world, as well as the different types of Islamic governments. *What Muslims Think, and How They Live* uses information collected in a landmark survey of the Islamic world by the Gallup Organization, as well as other socioeconomic data, to examine Muslim attitudes toward a variety of questions and issues.

As we enter a new century, cultural and political tensions between Muslims and non-Muslims continue. Now more than ever, it is important for people to learn more about their neighbors of all faiths. It is only through education and tolerance that we will be able to build a new world in which fear and mistrust are replaced with brotherhood and peace.

A painting by Rembrandt shows an angel intervening to stop Abraham from sacrificing his son. Muslims, Christians, and Jews revere Abraham as the first monotheist.

Father of Three Faiths

The knife glittered as Abraham, following the patterns of ancient ritual, prepared to make a sacrifice to his God. However, the creature lying bound on the altar before Abraham was no ordinary bull or sheep, such as might have been sacrificed as a burnt offering to one of the many pagan deities worshipped in the region known as the Fertile Crescent approximately 4,000 years ago. Abraham was spiritually different from the other people of his *polytheistic* culture; as a young man he had decided to obey a single God. Now, God had told Abraham to go into the mountains and sacrifice his young son.

It seems impossible that as Abraham raised the knife, he did not feel anxious at what he was about to do. Yet

9

the sources that describe the events of Abraham's life indicate that he was fully prepared to submit to the demands of his deity without question—even if that meant killing his own child.

This willingness to obey pleased God, who sent a messenger to stop Abraham before he could swing the knife downward. The request for sacrifice had been a test of Abraham's faith, one that he had passed. "Because you have done this and not withheld your son, your only son, I will surely bless you and make your descendants as numerous as the stars in the sky and the sand on the seashore," God promised Abraham. "Your descendants will take possession of the cities of their enemies, and through your offspring all nations on earth will be blessed, because you have obeyed me" (Genesis 22: 16–18).

This building, called a ziggurat, is located in Ur, once the most important city in Mesopotamia. Ziggurats were temples where the ancient Sumerians worshipped their gods; some scholars believe the ziggurat of Ur was dedicated to the moon god. This ziggurat was built around 2100 B.C.E. and therefore may have been seen by Abraham, who is believed to have spent the early years of his life in Ur.

Abraham is generally considered the first **monotheist**—a person who worships only one deity. The idea of a single, all-powerful God was a revolutionary concept that would change the world, ultimately spawning three important faiths: Judaism, Christianity, and Islam. Today the spiritual descendants of Abraham make up more than half of the world's population.

PRE-MONOTHEISTIC RELIGIOUS THOUGHT

No one can say exactly how or when religious thought first developed. The Jewish, Christian, and Muslim *scriptures* (the Torah, Bible, and Qur'an, respectively) agree that religious thought dates to the creation of the world, because Adam and Eve, the first man and woman in these scriptural traditions, communicated with God. Modern scientists have different ideas about how the earliest religious thought may have developed among prehistoric humans during the Stone Age, a period that stretches back as far as 2 million years.

Although it is impossible to know for certain how Stone Age humans lived and what they believed, there are generally accepted theories of behavior. Agriculture had not yet been developed, so humans had to hunt animals or gather wild fruits or grains. Humans spent all of their time trying to survive, so there was no time to develop the elements of civilization, such as written language or technology more advanced than simple tools made from stone or wood. Because people were constantly on the move, looking for new food sources or following wild animals, there were no cities or permanent settlements.

Like modern humans, people of the Stone Age understood the relationship between cause and effect. They knew, for example, that touching fire would cause a painful burn, or that eating the leaves of a particular plant would make them sick. However, there were many things prehistoric humans could not understand. What caused the sun to rise every morning and disappear each night? Why did thunder and lightning sometimes cause the forest to shake? To answer these types of questions, Stone Age people used their imaginations. They created stories to explain the forces of nature that they could not understand.

It is a short step from asking, "why does this happen?" to wondering "who or what caused this to happen?" People of the Stone Age came to believe that there were vital living forces, or spirits, everywhere in nature. People had spirits, which could be glimpsed when they saw their shimmering reflection in a pool of water. Trees, animals, rocks, rivers, and stars all had spirits. Good spirits caused dreams, and evil spirits brought illness. Angry spirits could express themselves through floods or storms.

Humans wanted to keep the spirits happy so they would protect the people and make their hunts successful. To do this, humans began to develop rituals intended to satisfy the spirits. Anthropologists consider the primitive myths about spirits, and the rituals created to appease them, to be the earliest expressions of religious thought. This type of religion is known as *animism*, and it is still practiced by people in some parts of Africa, South America, and Asia.

Human existence changed radically with the development of agriculture about 10,000 years ago. When humans learned to grow crops and raise domesticated livestock, they were able to control their food supply for the first time. This enabled them to settle in permanent communities. As farming became more efficient, it resulted in food surpluses, which in turn meant humans could devote more of their time to other pursuits, such as weaving cloth, making pottery, or working metal. As people living in these communities shared their knowledge and skills, the earliest civilizations began to develop.

The land between the Tigris and Euphrates Rivers is considered the site of the earliest civilization, Sumer. This area, later called Mesopotamia, is located in present-day Iraq. Great civilizations had already risen and fallen in this region by the time the patriarch Abraham was born here around the year 2000 B.C.E. And other early civilizations had emerged between 9,000 and 7,500 years

An ancient Egyptian temple. Some historians argue that an Egyptian pharaoh named Amenhotep IV (or Akhenaten), not the biblical patriarch Abraham, was the first true monotheist because while Abraham worshipped a single God, it is not clear that he denied the existence of other gods. Amenhotep, who ruled from 1375 to 1358 B.C.E., insisted that Egyptians worship only Ra, the sun god, and oversaw the destruction of temples to the other Egyptian deities. After his death, however, Egypt reverted to polytheism.

ago along the Nile River in Africa, in the Indus Valley in central Asia, and along the Yellow River in China.

Successful farming required rain for crops, fertile soil, good weather, and fresh water and grasses for livestock. If an unforeseen event—a river flood, a blight, an unexpected hailstorm—damaged the crops, many people would starve. Therefore appeasing the spirits—now called gods—became even more important. At one time a simple sacrifice might have sufficed. For example, a farmer whose field was threatened by a rising river might throw handfuls of grain into the waters to appease the river god. Eventually, though, humans developed sophisticated religious systems in which rituals and sacrifices were performed at certain times each year to ensure the fertility of crops. A class of priests was created to intercede with the gods and direct worship.

Humans worshipped many gods, whose names and the rituals required to please them varied greatly from place to place. People of these ancient cultures often worshipped gods that represented the sun, moon, or forces of nature. Major Sumerian gods—those the patriarch Abraham might have been familiar with, for example—included An, the god of the heavens; Ki, goddess of the earth; and their son Enlil, the god of air and storms. Egyptians generally worshipped Ra, the sun god, as creator of the universe, although some Egyptian traditions gave other gods the credit for creation.

THE IMPORTANCE OF MONOTHEISM

Abraham may have been a *henotheist*, rather than a true monotheist, as he is never said to have claimed there were no other gods. By tradition, however, he is considered the first human being to place himself completely in the hands of the one God. Because each of the gods worshipped by polytheists had separate and specific areas over which they had power, no single god could have the primary place in a person's life. Abraham, however, focused on the commands of a single deity, rather than on trying to appease all of the gods through various rituals. By doing this, Abraham placed the one supreme God at the center of his life.

Monotheism was a revolutionary idea because it radically changed the human perspective of the future. In the ancient world life and death were considered simply part of an endless cycle. Although the gods could intervene in human affairs, even the greatest of them were controlled by outside laws and forces. In the epic poem *The Iliad*, for example, Zeus is the greatest god of the Greek pantheon, but he cannot keep his mortal son Sarpedon from dying in battle because the Fates have decreed Sarpedon's death. Ancient humans were concerned primarily with the moments in which they lived; they did not have a concept of an afterlife, in which they would be held accountable for their earthly actions.

The *theology* that developed around worship of an all-powerful creator God, who controlled all aspects of nature and of human life, changed the way humans perceived the future. History came to be seen as linear, rather than cyclical, following a divine plan conceived by God. Thus time begins with God's creation of the world; time will eventually end, and God will judge each person's life.

Monotheists believe that through divine revelations to Abraham and others, God provided the laws by which He expected humans to live. The idea that God rewards or punishes people for their behavior led to the development of a new human ethical and moral code. Those who followed God's laws would be favored, but those who disobeyed would face severe consequences. As a result, in many places these laws became the basis for society, and they remain very much a part of the social order today.

"Whether you call it submission in Muslim terms, conversion in Christian terms, or *t'shuva* [turning toward God] for the Jews, monotheism is a radically new understanding," Eugene Fisher, the director of Catholic-Jewish relations for the U.S. Conference of Catholic Bishops, told *Time* magazine in 2002. "[It is] the underlying concept of Western civilization."

The illustrations on this page from a 14th-century manuscript depict events recorded in the Book of Genesis—God's creation of stars and animals, the creation of Eve, the Fall of Man, and Adam and Eve's expulsion from the Garden of Eden.

Shared Ancestors

The three major monotheistic religions share a similar view of the origins of humankind and the development of humans' relationship with God. Christians and Jews revere a group of ancient writings, which make up the first five books of both the Torah and the Christian Bible's Old Testament. The first of these writings, known in English as the Book of Genesis, describes how the world began. Muslims respect the authenticity of the Genesis teachings, and the Qur'an provides additional details about the biblical story of creation.

According to Genesis, God existed before all things, and He created the universe and everything in it. Genesis 1: 27 says, "God created man in his own image, in the image of God he created him; male and female he created them." Adam and Eve, the first man and woman in the Genesis account, live in a garden in Eden through which four rivers flow. They are given everything they need to be happy. God tells them they may eat the fruit of every tree except one: the tree of knowledge of good and evil. However, an evil spirit called Satan enters the garden in the form of a serpent. Satan encourages Adam and Eve to eat the fruit of the tree, which they do. God is angry when He finds that He has been disobeyed, and he expels Adam and Eve from Eden.

Christian theology holds that Adam and Eve's disobedience was the first sin, and that all of their human descendants were doomed to be born with the stain of this "original sin" on their souls. Humans, therefore, can be saved from their sins only through the intervention of Jesus Christ.

Jews and Muslims, however, do not accept the idea of original sin. Judaism teaches that redemption can be found through sincere repentance of sins and adherence to the commandments and laws God gave to Moses. Muslims believe that after Adam was expelled from the Garden of Eden, he repented and was forgiven. According to the second sura (chapter) of the Qur'an, God told Adam, "Surely there will come to you a guidance from Me, then whoever follows My guidance, no fear shall come upon them, nor shall they grieve" (Qur'an 2: 38). According to Muslim tradition, after being expelled from the garden Adam built the Kaaba as a place to worship God.

DISOBEDIENCE AND THE GREAT FLOOD

When Adam and Eve have children, "men began to call on the name of the Lord" (Genesis 4: 26). Unfortunately, according to scriptural accounts, later generations turn away from God and behave in ways that displease Him. Genesis 6: 11 says that the "earth was corrupt in God's sight and was full of violence." So God decides to destroy humankind, but spare the only good man on earth, along with his family. God tells that man, Noah, to build an enormous boat, called an ark, explaining:

> I am going to bring floodwaters on the earth to destroy all life under the heavens. . . . Everything on earth will perish. But I will establish my covenant with you, and you will enter the ark—you and your sons and your wife and your son's wives with you. You are to bring into the ark two of all living creatures, male and female, to keep them alive with you. Two of every kind of bird, of every kind of animal and of every kind of creature that moves along the ground will come to you to be kept alive. (Genesis 6: 17–20)

Noah does as God has commanded, and when the ark is ready, the Great Flood commences. The Bible says that it rained for 40 days and 40 nights, and that the earth was flooded for 150 days. After the waters finally recede, Noah, his family, and the animals leave the ark. Noah builds an altar and makes a sacrifice to God;

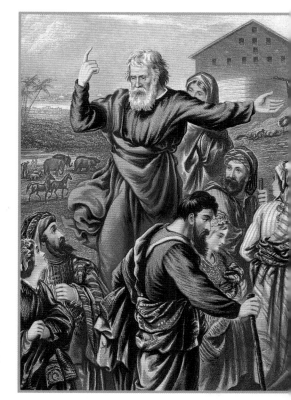

As animals stream into the ark behind him, Noah encourages his family to hurry into the shelter before the Great Flood begins. Many Middle Eastern cultures recorded stories about a flood that destroyed the entire earth. One of these, the Epic of Gilgamesh, pre-dates the Book of Genesis; the epic was written in ancient Sumer between 2700 and 2500 B.C.E.

this pleases God, who in return promises that He will never again send a flood to destroy the earth.

The story of Noah is also a part of Islamic scriptures, and Muslims revere Noah as a great messenger. The Islamic account relates that, in addition to his family and the animals, Noah is also allowed to save a group of friends who believe in God. As the waters are rising, Noah sees one of his sons, who has not entered the ark, and he urges the young man to join him with the other believers. Noah's son refuses, saying that he will instead climb to the highest mountains where the water cannot reach. Because he does not believe, he is lost.

After the Great Flood, according to the Bible, Noah's three surviving sons spread out to inhabit the entire earth. The descendants of Shem, Noah's oldest son, became known as the Semites. The Semites settled throughout the region today known as the Middle East, from Syria to the Arabian Peninsula. Today, the Semitic peoples include both ethnic Jews and Arabs. The Hamitic peoples, descended from Noah's son Ham, lived in Africa, as well as in the land known as Canaan along the Mediterranean Sea. The descendants of Japheth inhabited both Asia and Europe; the Japhethites are said to include Greeks, Celts, the Germanic tribes, Persians, Indians, and many other ancient peoples.

Noah and the people on the ark, the scriptures relate, were saved because they believed in God, but eventually Noah's descendants again turn to other gods. Many generations after Noah, God speaks to a descendant of Shem, who listens and obeys. This man's name is Abram, but God eventually changes it to Abraham, which means "father of many," because his descendants will become so numerous.

THE LIFE OF ABRAHAM

Abram is generally said to have lived sometime between 2200 and 1800 B.C.E. (That Abram was a historical figure is a matter of faith, as conclusive archaeological evidence of his existence has

This map shows Abraham's travels, according to Muslim, Christian, and Jewish sources. All three faiths agree that he left Ur and journeyed north to Haran, then southwest into Egypt and back to Canaan, and that he is buried in Hebron. Muslims believe Abraham often traveled south into the Arabian Peninsula to visit his son Ishmael.

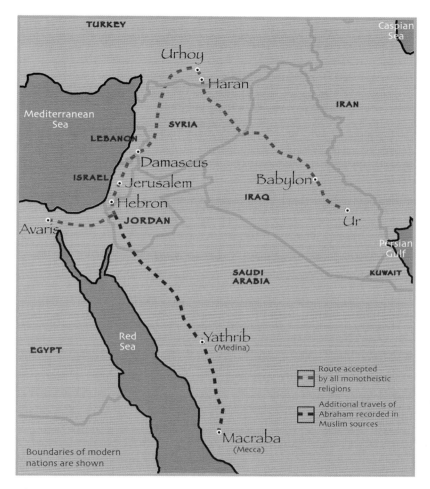

not been found, and the earliest references to him are in scriptural accounts that were written long after he is said to have lived.) Genesis says that he was born in a city called Ur of the Chaldeans, which is traditionally thought to be the ancient city of Ur in Mesopotamia (in present-day Iraq). The story of his life is an important part of the Book of Genesis, but he is also mentioned numerous times in other Jewish and Christian writings, as well as in the Qur'an.

There are numerous Muslim and Jewish stories about Abram's childhood. According to a Jewish tale, Abram's father, Terah, made and sold idols to the people of Ur. One day when young Abram was alone in his father's shop, he smashed all of the idols except the largest one. When his father returned and saw what had happened, Abram blamed the destruction on the surviving idol. This showed him the folly of worshipping immovable idols made of stone. The Qur'an agrees that Abram admonished his father for making idols; there is also a Muslim story that a ruler threw the young man into a fire when he refused to worship the gods, but that Abram came out unharmed.

The Bible says that Abram married a woman named Sarai, and that eventually they left Ur. Taking Abram's father and his nephew Lot, they moved north to Haran, a city located in present-day Turkey. They settled there for a time, but when Abram was 75 years old God told him, "Leave your country, your people, and your father's household and go to the land I will show you" (Genesis 12: 1). This marked an important decision for Abram: should he give up a comfortable life in exchange for an unknown future? How could Abram be sure God would protect him? What if there were stronger gods that wanted to hurt him when he left Haran?

The scriptures do not indicate whether Abram had any doubts, only that he obeyed, moving west with Sarai, Lot, and their possessions. Genesis describes Abram's travels through Canaan to Egypt and back to Canaan, where he settled. Abram prospered in Canaan and became respected as both a military leader and a peacemaking diplomat. According to one story in Genesis, when Abram's nephew Lot was captured by enemies, Abram and his men went after them. They won the battle and rescued Lot. As Abram was returning home, he met the king of Salem and a "priest of God Most High," Melchizedek, who gave Abram bread, wine, and a blessing. Salem is traditionally believed to be the place where a great city would eventually be built: Jerusalem.

THE COVENANT

Throughout Genesis, God promises that as long as Abram obeys, He will make Abram's descendants a great nation—as numerous as the dust of the earth or the stars in the sky. This promise is known as the **covenant**—a solemn and binding agreement between two parties.

However, Abram doubts that what God has promised will come to pass. After all, he and Sarai have never had children, and now Sarai is too old. So Sarai permits her 86-year-old husband to impregnate her servant, an Egyptian woman named Hagar. When Hagar conceives and bears a son named Ishmael ("God hears"), Abram has an heir.

Thirteen years later, God again speaks to Abram. This time, He tells Abram that as a symbol of the covenant, he and all of his male descendants must be circumcised. God changes Abram's name to Abraham and 90-year-old Sarai's name to Sarah. He also promises that she will bear Abraham's child.

Abraham and Ishmael are circumcised, as God has demanded, and so are all of the other men in their camp. Nine months later Sarah gives birth to a son, whom she names Isaac ("He laughs"). When Isaac is eight days old he too is circumcised.

Once Sarah has her own child, she wants to make sure Isaac, not Ishmael, will inherit Abraham's possessions. She forces Abraham to send Hagar and Ishmael away from the camp. This event marks an important divergence between the Judeo-Christian and the Muslim traditions. According to Genesis, God tells Abraham to let Hagar and Ishmael leave because "it is through Isaac that your offspring will be reckoned." Alone in the desert, Hagar and Ishmael give up hope, but God saves them and promises Hagar that Ishmael's descendants will become a great nation. Genesis says that God was with Ishmael as he grew up. The Qur'an supplements this story by explaining that Hagar and Ishmael made their way to the Arabian Peninsula, where the angel Gabriel created a well of fresh water for them called Zamzam. They lived in a small house near the Kaaba, where Abraham often visited them. The Kaaba had been destroyed in the Great Flood, so Abraham and Ishmael together rebuilt the ancient shrine.

In Genesis, God's command that Abraham sacrifice his son comes after Hagar and Ishmael are sent away, and it is Isaac—

This elaborate miniature painting depicts Abraham's attempt to obey God's command and sacrifice his son; the angel pictured at the right is carrying a sheep for him to sacrifice instead. Muslims consider Abraham the spiritual father of all who believe in God. Sura 22, verse 78 of the Qur'an says, "Strive hard for Allah with due striving. He has chosen you and has not laid upon you any hardship in your religion, the faith of your father Abraham."

through whom the Jewish people trace their lineage—who is to be sacrificed. According to tradition the sacrifice was to occur on the Temple Mount in Jerusalem.

This is another point at which the Islamic tradition diverges. Muslims believe that Ishmael—from whom the Arabs claim descent—was the son whom Abraham intended to sacrifice, and that this event occurred near the Kaaba before Isaac was even born. When Abraham passed God's test, the Qur'an says, he was told that he would be given another son, Isaac, "a prophet from among the righteous ones" (Qur'an 37: 102).

This is an important point, and one on which all three religions differ. Jews believe that the covenant between God and Abraham is passed on to them through Isaac. Therefore they are God's "chosen people," and as long as they keep the covenant they will be blessed.

Although Islam teaches that God's blessing was passed through Ishmael, rather than Isaac, Muslims also believe that the covenant with God is determined by their faith, rather than their genealogy. The chosen people of God are those who submit to His will.

Like the Jews, Christians believe Abraham was told to sacrifice Isaac, rather than Ishmael. However, like the Muslims, Christians believe that their faith, rather than their lineage, makes them God's chosen people. Early Christian leaders used Abraham as an example that all people—not just the Jews—could be part of the community of believers. "It was not through [Jewish] law that Abraham and his offspring received the promise that he would be heir of the world, but through the righteousness that comes by faith," wrote the apostle Paul in his letter to the Romans. "For if those who live by law are heirs, faith has no value and the promise is worthless. . . . Therefore the promise comes by faith, so that it may be by grace and may be guaranteed to all Abraham's off-spring—not only to those who are of the law but also to those who are of the faith of Abraham. He is the father of us all" (Romans 4: 13–14, 16).

ORIGINS OF THE HEBREWS

Abraham is said to have remained in Canaan after making the covenant with God. Genesis 25: 9 says that when he died, he was buried by both Ishmael and Isaac. Ishmael's descendants are then listed; Genesis 25: 18 says that they "settled in the area from Havilah to Shur, near the border of Egypt, as you go toward Asshur. And they lived in hostility toward all their brothers."

Genesis continues with stories about Abraham's son Isaac and Isaac's son Jacob and his descendants. These people are often called either Hebrews or Israelites. The origin of *Hebrew*, the older term, is uncertain; it may be derived from the word *hiberu*, which is found in ancient Egyptian writings and is believed to mean "wanderer" or "outsider." The word *Israelites* comes from Israel, a name given to Abraham's grandson Jacob. According to Genesis 32: 22–32, one night Jacob wrestles with an angel of God and refuses to let the angel go. In the morning, the angel renames him Israel, which means "he struggles with God."

Israel and his family migrate throughout Canaan in search of good pastureland for their herds of livestock. They share the land with many other people, known collectively as the Canaanites. Among these people are the descendants of Israel's twin brother, Esau, who become known as the Edomites.

Israel and his wife, Rachel, have 12 sons. Genesis says that Israel's sons became jealous of their youngest brother, Joseph, because he was his father's favorite. One day, the 11 older brothers sell Joseph to slave traders. To explain his disappearance, the older brothers tell their father that a wild animal has killed Joseph.

God watches over Joseph, however. He is taken to Egypt, where he becomes a servant of the pharaoh. With God's help, Joseph rises from his humble position to a rank second only to that of the pharaoh himself. God warns Joseph that a seven-year famine is coming, so the Egyptians have time to store enough food to survive.

Canaan is also hit by famine, but the people there have not prepared for it. To keep his family from starving, Joseph invites them to Egypt, where there is plenty of food. Israel and his sons do not know why they have been asked to come, but Joseph eventually reveals himself to them. The brothers are afraid Joseph might seek retribution after their father's death, but Joseph promises forgiveness. According to Genesis 50: 20–21, Joseph tells them, "You intended to harm me, but God intended it for good to accomplish what is now being done, the saving of many lives. So then, don't be afraid."

The Israelites would remain in Egypt long after the deaths of Joseph and his brothers. The scriptures say the people were in Egypt for 430 years. Unfortunately, their good situation eventually turned bad when a new pharaoh came to power. Fearing that the Israelites had grown too numerous, he enslaved them and put them to work in the fields and on building projects.

The Hebrew Bible says that the Israelites lived in Egypt for 430 years. After they were enslaved they may have been put to work building pyramids or other Egyptian monuments commissioned by the pharaohs.

According to popular tradition, the Israelites provided the labor to build some of Egypt's great pyramids and monuments. The scriptures merely state, "The Israelites groaned in their slavery and cried out, and their cry for help because of their slavery went up to God. God heard their groaning and he remembered his covenant with Abraham, with Isaac, and with Jacob. So God looked on the Israelites and was concerned about them" (Exodus 2: 23–25).

God decides to help the Israelites escape from slavery in Egypt, by encouraging a leader named Moses to speak to the pharaoh. The pharaoh initially refuses to let the Israelites go, but after God has performed many signs and wonders, he relents.

For the next 40 years, the Israelites wander through the desert of Sinai, and during this time God establishes a new covenant with them. The laws and commandments that God gives to Moses in the desert form the basis of a religion that will one day become known as Judaism.

A group of Jews in traditional dress participate in a ceremony in Israel. The ornate scroll on the table contains the Torah, or first five books of the Hebrew Bible, the basis for Jewish law and custom.

Origins of Judaism

The Tanakh, or Hebrew Bible, is the holy scriptures of Judaism. The Tanakh includes 39 books, which were written between 3,100 and 2,400 years ago, although many draw on earlier oral traditions. The Tanakh includes books about Israel's greatest prophets, such as Samuel, Isaiah, and Jeremiah, and great writings such as Psalms and Proverbs. But the most important part of the Tanakh is the Torah, or first five books: Genesis, Exodus, Leviticus, Numbers, and Deuteronomy. These books are attributed to Moses, although they were preserved orally and not written down until much later. The Torah contains stories about the creation of humankind, the early history of the Israelites and their covenant with God, and the laws and commandments that God expected them to obey.

"There has been no book in the history of the West that has done more to shape the ideologies, theologies, and other belief systems by which we live," writes George Robinson in *Essential Judaism*. "For better and worse, the Hebrew Bible has served not only as the founding myth of Judaism but also as the base from which Christianity and Islam evolved. There is no major Western religion that does not owe its existence in some way to the Hebrew Bible." (It should be noted that Muslims do not believe Christianity and Islam evolved from Judaism, but rather that all three messages were with God from eternity, and He simply revealed them at different times, to different prophets, and in different languages.)

Moses is arguably the greatest human figure in Judaism, but he is

Moses, who led the Israelites out of Egypt, is a major figure in the development of Judaism. While the Israelites were camped in the desert, the Book of Exodus says, God spoke to Moses on top of a nearby mountain and gave him the Ten Commandments, which were engraved on stone tablets. But when Moses returned to the Israelite camp, he found the people worshipping a golden idol, so he angrily smashed the tablets, representing the breaking of the covenant. God later gave Moses a new set of tablets engraved with the laws.

presented in the Torah as a flawed leader who is reluctant to serve as God's messenger to the pharaoh because he fears that he will not be up to the task. Yet Moses ultimately accepts, and with God's help he performs signs and wonders for the pharaoh. The obstinate ruler refuses to let the Israelites leave Egypt, even as the signs become more intense, until finally God sends a devastating plague: in one night, all of the first-born male children of Egypt are killed. First, however, God tells the Israelites how to prepare so the angel of death will pass over their houses. (This night is remembered in one of the most important Jewish festivals: Pesach, or Passover.) After this devastating blow, the Israelites are permitted to leave Egypt.

Led by Moses and his brother Aaron, the Israelites wander homeless in the Sinai desert for 40 years. During this time, God makes a new covenant with the Israelites. According to Exodus 19: 3-8:

> Then Moses went up to God, and the Lord called to him from the mountain and said, "This is what you are to say to the house of Jacob and what you are to tell the people of Israel: 'You yourselves have seen what I did to Egypt, and how I carried you on eagle's wings and brought you to myself. Now if you obey me fully and keep my covenant, then out of all nations you will be my treasured possession. Although the whole earth is mine, you will be for me a kingdom of priests and a holy nation.' These are the words you are to speak to the Israelites."

> So Moses went back and summoned the elders of the people and set before them all the words the Lord had commanded him to speak. The people all responded together, "We will do everything the Lord has said." So Moses brought their answer back to the Lord.

God then gives Moses the Ten Commandments, the first two of which illustrate the importance of monotheism and obedience to God in Judaism: "I am the Lord, your God . . . You shall have no other gods before me" and "You shall not bow down to [idols] or worship them." God also gives Moses more than 600 laws for the Israelites to follow. When the Israelites agree to live by these laws, God promises to give them possession of Canaan, as a place where they can establish their nation. The Israelites will have to fight the

Canaanites for the land, although God will be with them as long as they remain faithful to Him.

ISRAEL'S RISE AND FALL

When the Israelites arrived in Canaan around 1500 B.C.E., the Canaanites had a sophisticated civilization. Most Canaanite cities were located on the coast of the Mediterranean Sea, making them natural centers for trade and the exchange of knowledge and technology. This gave the Canaanites access to iron tools and weapons, while the Israelites had lower-quality weapons made of softer bronze. Despite this disadvantage, the scriptures say that with God's help, the Israelites gained quick victories over Jericho and other strong Canaanite towns.

The scriptures also relate how God assigned different areas of land to each of the 12 Israelite tribes. He told the Israelites to completely destroy the Canaanites and possess the entire land. This brutal directive has troubled some people, who have wondered how a just and merciful God could sanction such annihilation. Theologians speculate that God wanted to keep his chosen people away from the influence of the Canaanites, who worshipped strange but seductive gods that might tempt the Israelites into behavior that would violate their covenant.

In any case, although the Israelites did take control of the land and massacre many people, they did not obey God completely. Some Canaanites were enslaved; others defended their territories or made treaties with the Israelites. The ultimate conquest of Canaan would take several hundred years. Also, as the Israelites observed Canaanite rituals and intermarried into their families, the people began to turn away from God and worshipped the gods revered by their pagan neighbors.

For much of the time the Israelites were fighting for Canaan, wise heroes known as the Judges ruled the people. When the Israelites turned away from God, judges like Deborah, Gideon, and Samson helped bring them back to the true path. Eventually, however, the people of Israel decided that they, like other nations, wanted a king to rule over them. A man named Saul was anointed the first king of Israel; he ruled from about 1022 to 1000 B.C.E. After Saul was killed in battle, a young man named David became king.

During the reign of King David (1000–961 B.C.E.), Israel achieved its greatest glory. David captured the city of Jerusalem and made it his capital. David's kingdom covered the area of the modern-day state of Israel, as well as parts of Lebanon, Syria, Jordan, and Iraq. This was a time in ancient history when the traditional world powers, empires based in Mesopotamia and Egypt, were comparatively weak; as a result Israel, located between these two lands, emerged as the dominant power of its day.

David's son Solomon was considered a wise ruler who maintained the powerful position of Israel. Solomon is also credited with building the enormous Holy Temple in Jerusalem where God was worshipped. But after Solomon's death around 922 B.C.E., the kingdom

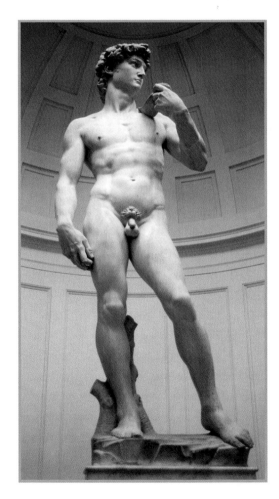

Michelangelo's famous sculpture of David depicts the future king as a young man, during the time of his fight with Goliath. In the statue's hands are a rock and sling, the weapons David used to defeat the giant Philistine warrior. David would become Israel's greatest king; he is described in the Hebrew Bible as "a man after God's own heart."

became divided. The kingdom of Judah was established in the southern part of the country and included the tribes of Judah and Benjamin. The kingdom of Israel, or Northern Kingdom, included the other 10 tribes; its capital was at the city of Samaria.

Scripture relates that some of the kings who ruled over the two Israelite kingdoms remained faithful to God and His commandments, but that most of the rulers—and most of the people—disobeyed God. In 722 B.C.E. the Northern Kingdom was conquered by the powerful Assyrians, and the 10 tribes were dispersed and lost to history. The Jewish people interpreted this calamity as God's punishment for their breaking of the covenant.

In the remaining Israelite kingdom of Judah, prophets such as Isaiah and Jeremiah reminded the people and their leaders about the importance of keeping their covenant with God and admonished them to give up their wicked ways. Scripture relates that the Israelites did not listen to the prophets, however. In 586 B.C.E. the Babylonians conquered Judah, taking the capital of Jerusalem and destroying the Holy Temple there. Many of the Israelites were taken as prisoners to Babylon.

JUDAISM DEVELOPS IN EXILE

During the captivity in Babylon, the Israelites' religion underwent significant changes. It was at this point that the religion began to be referred to as Judaism, and the people who practiced it as Jews.

Since the time of Solomon the Temple had been a focal point where the entire Israelite community came to worship God and perform the rituals of sacrifice. With the Temple destroyed and the Israelites in exile, several prophets appeared and explained that no matter where the people were, they could establish a relationship with God on an individual and personal basis.

Perhaps most important, the exile forced the Israelites to reconsider their view of God. In the past, they had worshipped God while at the same time considering the deities of other nations legitimate—and sometimes even worshipping other gods as well. In Babylon the prophets taught that God controlled all of history, and that there were no other gods or forces that could affect their lives. If the Israelites kept the covenant, the prophets taught, God would save His people from captivity and reestablish a kingdom that would be greater than King David's.

The Jewish communities in Babylon became centered in places of communal prayer, where the priests could teach the laws of the covenant and perform worship ceremonies. These eventually became known as synagogues, and they would become a vital part of Jewish religious life. The synagogues came to be led by teachers known as rabbis.

Babylonian rule ended in 539 B.C.E. when the Persians crushed Babylon. Although the Persian ruler Cyrus the Great gave Jews permission to return to Jerusalem, many remained in Babylon. These Jews established themselves in Persian society and business but maintained their religious beliefs.

Tens of thousands of Jews did leave Babylon after 539 and returned to Jerusalem and the surrounding area. Cyrus had ordered them to rebuild the Temple, and the Jews enthusiastically began this project. However, they found themselves fighting people living in northern Canaan, including the Samaritans—descendants of Israelites who had remained in the land after the Babylonian invasion and had intermarried with pagans. This delayed the reconstruction of the Temple, which was not completed for more than 20 years.

In 458 B.C.E. a priest named Ezra led a second group of Jews from Babylon to Jerusalem. On his arrival, Ezra told the Jews of Jerusalem that they needed to be more careful to follow the law. He undertook a program of regularly reading the law to the people and explaining how the Jews should behave. Through Ezra's actions the Jews realized that many of God's laws had not been kept for centuries. For example, the Israelites were supposed to observe a certain festival during the seventh month of the year—the Festival of Tabernacles, or Sukkot. However, the ceremonies had not been performed correctly since shortly after the time of Moses. The Book of Nehemiah says that after Ezra taught the people about the law, they observed the festival properly.

Determining exactly how God wanted the Jews to observe His commandments became an important element of Judaism. Priests began to teach the people how the laws should be interpreted and obeyed. From this developed an elaborate legal code of conduct for the Jews to follow. This code was unwritten, because the Jewish priests did not want to imply that their rulings could not change or that they were the equals of God's laws as presented in the Torah. Instead, the priests memorized the laws and the cases that had led to different rulings, passing this information orally to later generations.

The Macedonian ruler Alexander the Great was the greatest conqueror of ancient times. Alexander and his successors spread Greek influence throughout the Mediterranean world and into Asia. Hellenism would have a great impact on the development and spread of Judaism.

THE IMPACT OF HELLENISM

In 334 B.C.E., Macedonian and Greek armies led by Alexander the Great invaded Persian-controlled territories. By 332 Alexander's forces controlled the Jewish territories on the eastern Mediterranean seacoast, and within 10 years Alexander ruled a vast empire that stretched from Egypt in the west to India in the east. Alexander's conquests had an immediate and lasting impact on the Mediterranean world. The language and practices of the Greeks became dominant throughout his empire.

The blending of Alexander's Greek culture with aspects of the conquered Persian and Asian cultures became known as Hellenism. During the Hellenistic period, trade increased between different regions. This led to a sharing of scientific and religious ideas. Greek became the language of aristocrats and intellectuals. Many Jews, particularly those who were wealthy or educated, admired Greek schools and libraries, philosophical and logical systems, and art. Some Jews adopted Greek dress and accepted Greek names.

After Alexander's sudden death in 323, his enormous empire was divided among four rulers. Cassander ruled Greece, Lysimachus controlled Asia Minor and Thrace, Seleucus I Nicator had power over Mesopotamia and Syria, and Ptolemy I Soter governed the Mediterranean coast and Egypt. Their descendants continued to fight over the territory. By 281 B.C.E., there were two major ruling families: the Seleucids, who ruled the territory north of Syria, and the Ptolemies, who ruled the eastern Mediterranean and south to Egypt.

Under Persian rule, the two major Jewish communities had been centered in Jerusalem and Babylon. The Greeks, however, built many new cities throughout their empire, and Jews were considered ideal settlers. The Greek rulers moved large groups of Jews to such new cities as Alexandria and Antioch.

Initially, the Jewish people thrived under Greek rule. The Jews traditionally had been farmers and herders, but Jews who moved to the cities became part of the growing mercantile class. Jews also had special privileges within the empire. They did not have to worship the emperor as other Greeks did, and they did not have to serve in the military because they refused to work or fight on the Sabbath. Instead of paying a tax to the empire, Jews paid a tax toward upkeep of the Temple in Jerusalem. The Jews of Jerusalem also had a certain degree of autonomy within the empire, and Jewish (rather than Greek) law remained the basis for government in the city.

During this time a Greek translation of the Hebrew Bible, called the Septuagint, was created; this meant the holy text was now accessible to people who could not speak Hebrew. The availability of the Septuagint text helped spread interest in Judaism, and many Greek-speaking people converted to the religion. The population of Judea—as the area corresponding to the territory of the former kingdom of Judah was now called—stood at about 100,000 at the time of Alexander; within four centuries it is estimated that a million Jews lived in Palestine and another 2 million in Egypt and Syria.

In 198 B.C.E. the Seleucids displaced the Ptolemies as rulers of Judea. This would lead to greater tension between the Jews and the Greeks. In 175 the Seleucid emperor appointed a new Jewish high priest, Jason, who in turn agreed to let Jerusalem become a *polis*, or Greek city. This allowed Greek laws and customs to replace Jewish ones. Gradually, this led to a division among the Jews. Some, particularly in the wealthier classes, enthusiastically embraced Hellenism. There are stories of Jews who had their circumcisions undone through a painful surgical procedure so that they could become Greek citizens. Other Jews were appalled at Greek practices, many of which were antithetical to the values of the Torah, and they began to oppose the spread of Hellenistic culture in Judea.

Eventually, the Seleucid emperor Antiochus IV Epiphanes imposed harsh new restrictions on the residents of Jerusalem. He forbade Jews to observe the Sabbath or perform circumcisions, and he erected a statue of himself in the Temple. The emperor's demand to be worshipped as a god was unacceptable, and in 168 B.C.E. a priest named Mattathias and his sons rose up in protest. After four years of fighting, Jewish forces under Judah Maccabee captured Jerusalem, and in December 164 they rededicated the Temple.

"The Maccabean revolt was a critical turning point in the history of Judaism," writes Daniel Jeremy Silver in *A History of Judaism*. "It resulted in an unexpected victory for the traditionalists. Because of it the Torah remained the uncontested constitution of Jerusalem."

The Hasmoneans, descendants of Mattathias, established themselves as kings of an independent Judea. But Mattathias had been only a minor religious leader, not a descendant of the high priests of the Temple. To interpret Jewish law and assist the Hasmonean ruler a new council, the Sanhedrin, was formed to have jurisdiction over religious matters as well as civil and criminal cases.

A menorah with eight branches is lit each year during Hanukkah, the eight-day-long Jewish Festival of Lights. Hanukkah celebrates a miracle that occurred during the rededication of the Temple in 164 B.C.E. Jews under Judah Maccabee captured the Temple after several years of fighting against the Seleucid rulers of Jerusalem. A Jewish state was established, but its independence would last less than a century.

ROMAN RULE AND RABBINIC JUDAISM

Judean self-rule would last only until 63 B.C.E., when the Roman Empire claimed Judea as a province. The Romans first installed puppet monarchs (the most famous of these was King Herod), and then sent Roman governors (procurators) to rule Judea.

Roman rule was unpopular. Rome resorted to harsh measures when necessary to maintain control over its vast territories, and it imposed heavy taxes on its subjects. At various times Jews organized into groups to oppose Rome; in response, Roman legions were garrisoned in Jerusalem and elsewhere to prevent rebellion.

Two revolts had dire consequences for the Jews. The first began in 66 C.E. In the year 70 the Romans laid siege to and eventually sacked Jerusalem, in the process destroying the Holy Temple, massacring thousands of Jews, and taking thousands of others into captivity. A second revolt, led by Simon bar Kokhba, erupted in 132. Years of difficult fighting ensued before the Romans finally prevailed in 135. After this, Roman legions destroyed Jerusalem, forced most Jews to leave the land, and renamed the region Palestine.

Important developments in Judaism ensured the religion's survival after these disasters. During the rule of the Hasmoneans, two groups with opposing points of view had competed for preeminence within Judaism. On one side were the Sadducees, who believed in strict adherence to the written Torah law and wanted to see power again consolidated in the hands of the high priests. The other group was the Pharisees, who believed that both oral and written traditions should be used to interpret the law and felt that rabbis should have a greater role in leading their religious communities. This point of view came to dominate Judaism by the second century C.E.

Throughout the Roman period—and particularly after the destruction of the Temple—Pharisee rabbis produced a large amount of written interpretation of both the Torah and the oral law. When the Temple was destroyed and the population dispersed, the synagogues were again the center of Jewish religious life. It became even more important that each community's rabbi have a complete understanding of God's law.

Most of the law had never been written down; instead, it was carried in the memories of the Temple priests and handed down from generation to generation. Without the Temple as a unifying element, the Pharisees feared that the law and Judaism's oral

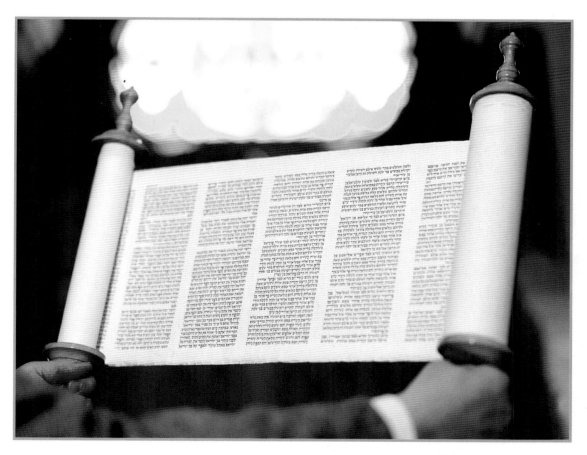

For generations the Jewish high priests, who came from the tribe of Levi, preserved the laws and their proper interpretation. During the time of the Hasmoneans and the subsequent Roman occupation of Judea, however, Jewish laws began to be written down to ensure that the enormous body of information and tradition would be preserved. This would help Judaism survive as a unified religion after the destruction of the Temple by Roman troops in 70 C.E.

traditions might be lost. In the first century C.E., religious leaders agreed on the written scriptures that belonged in the Hebrew Bible; after this no books could be added to the canon. Around 200 C.E. a rabbi known as Judah the Prince collected and edited the oral law into a text that became known as the Mishnah.

The Mishnah preserved just the oral law, without providing citations from the scriptures to explain the law. Over a period of several hundred years Jewish scholars who had memorized and studied the Torah and Mishnah would create a new text to explain the relationship between the oral law and the Torah. This enormous commentary on the law was called the Talmud, from a Hebrew word that means "learning." Two Jewish communities created Talmuds independently: one in Babylon, the other to the north of Jerusalem.

The Torah, Mishnah, and Talmud created an authoritative written body of Jewish law and custom (*halachah*). As a result, even during the Diaspora (the dispersal of the Jewish community) all Jews could look to the *halachah* for guidance. This ensured that Judaism would remain the same no matter where it was practiced, as all rabbis could draw on the same written sources to teach their congregations.

Thus the development of Rabbinic Judaism gave lasting strength to the Jewish faith, saving Judaism from being lost to history like many other ancient religions. Over the centuries the practice of Judaism would undergo changes, and by the 19th century the Reform and Conservative branches of the faith had emerged. Despite changing interpretation, however, the Torah, Mishnah, and Talmud remain the cornerstones of Judaism.

Although Judaism is a complex faith, a simple story provides insight into its essence. One day about 2,000 years ago, a non-Jew asked the great teacher Rabbi Hillel to quickly teach him as much about Judaism as he could. "What is hateful to you, do not do to your neighbor," Hillel said. "This is the whole of Jewish Law; the rest is commentary. Now go and study it."

There were alternative movements to Rabbinic Judaism in Rabbi Hillel's time. Most of these movements for reform or change died out, but one sect would survive and ultimately thrive. As Judaism turned inward to establish the laws that would protect the religion from misinterpretation, this sect would spread outward, eventually becoming the dominant religion of the Roman world.

The Church of the Agony in Jerusalem was built over the spot on the Mount of Olives where, according to tradition, Jesus prayed on the night before he was arrested and crucified.

The Birth of Christianity

As subjects of Babylonian, Persian, Greek, and Roman rulers, Jews longed for the establishment of a new Jewish state in which they would be free from oppression. Many Jewish prophets—from Isaiah, who lived during the Babylonian exile, to Daniel, whose writings dated to the end of the Hellenistic period—had predicted that one day a great leader from the line of King David would come and establish a kingdom even greater than ancient Israel. This priest-king would be the *moshiach*, or Messiah, the savior of the Jews.

Approximately 2,000 years ago, while Judea languished as a Roman province, a man named Jesus appeared in the Galilee region to the north of

Jerusalem. Jesus was a Jew who had grown up in the small town of Nazareth, and when he was about 30 years old he began to preach a message of reform and repentance. He emphasized the importance of obeying God's law, but encouraged Jews to focus on spiritual matters and the glorification of God.

As Jesus spoke publicly and performed miracles throughout Judea, he attracted a substantial group of followers. From this group he selected 12 as his apostles, and he spent the better part of three years teaching them. The apostles came to believe Jesus was the Messiah, but they apparently missed the point of his teaching. They thought he had come to free them from Rome. Instead, Jesus explained, he was the Son of God and had come to save humankind from its sins.

The Jewish tradition taught that humans had sinned since the time of Adam. Jews believed that when they violated the laws of Moses, their sins could be forgiven if they participated in certain rituals of atonement. Jesus argued that many Jews, particularly the Pharisees, placed too much emphasis on carefully following the forms established by law and tradition, and not enough on true repentance. God was angered by pride but pleased by humble penitence and service to others, Jesus taught.

Though Jesus said that Jewish law must still be observed, his teaching added to God's requirements, making them even more difficult. For example, he taught, "You have heard that it was said, 'Love you neighbor and hate your enemy.' But I tell you: Love your enemies and pray for those who persecute you, that you may be sons of your Father in heaven" (Mathew 5: 43–45). His followers were told not to fight back when attacked and to share what they had with others.

Jewish leaders disagreed with Jesus' teachings and were offended that he claimed to be the Son of God. When Jesus and the apostles visited Jerusalem for the annual Jewish Passover celebration, members of the Sanhedrin collaborated with Roman authorities to have Jesus arrested as a threat to Rome. Jesus submitted to arrest without resisting, and after being humiliated and tortured, he suffered an agonizing death through crucifixion—a Roman method of execution in which the prisoner was nailed to a wooden cross through the wrists and feet, and, after several hours of intense pain, generally died of suffocation. The exact date is uncertain, but Jesus' crucifixion is believed to have occurred around 29 C.E.

Crucifixion should have been the end of the story, but amazingly, it was only the beginning. Three days later, according to his followers, Jesus rose from the grave. Scripture relates that over the next 40 days, Jesus appeared to his disciples on many occasions. During this period of extended teaching, they came to understand that God had sent His son Jesus as the ultimate sacrifice to redeem sinful humanity.

Years earlier, on first seeing Jesus at the start of his public ministry, a prophet named John the Baptist had proclaimed, "Look, the Lamb of God, who takes away the sins of the world!" (John 1:

The word *redeem* means to pay back a debt; Christians believe that Jesus suffered and died on the cross in order to redeem the sins of humanity.

29). This was a reference to a temple ritual in which an unblemished lamb was sacrificed to atone for sins. The significance of John's words was that Jesus—unblemished by original sin and sinless in his life—would atone for the sins of all humanity through his sacrifice on the cross. Anyone who accepted Jesus and his teachings would have his or her sins forgiven and could develop a closer relationship with God.

The Gospels—scriptural accounts of Jesus' life and ministry—record that Jesus had taught this before his death, but his 12 chosen apostles had not understood. In a passage from John's Gospel, Jesus explains:

> For God so loved the world that he gave his one and only Son, that whoever believes in him shall not perish but have eternal life. For God did not send his Son into the world to condemn the world, but to save the world through him. Whoever believes in him is not condemned, but whoever does not believe stands condemned already because he has not believed in the name of God's one and only Son. This is the verdict: Light has come into the world, but men loved the darkness instead of light because their deeds were evil. Everyone who does evil hates the light, and will not come into the light for fear that his deeds will be exposed. But whoever lives by the truth comes into the light, so that it may be seen plainly that what he has done has been done through God. (John 3: 16–21)

At the end of the 40-day period of teaching, the Acts of the Apostles relates, Jesus told his closest disciples to spread his message to all humankind. He promised them the assistance of the Holy Spirit, which God would send to inspire their ministry. He then ascended into heaven, and his apostles went out to spread the message of salvation. The people who accepted Jesus as their savior came to be called Christians, a word derived from *Christos*, the Greek term for "Messiah."

THE EARLY CHRISTIAN CHURCH

The Gospels—the four books in the Christian New Testament that detail the life and ministry of Jesus—were written several decades after Jesus' death. A Christian missionary named Mark wrote the first gospel (the Gospel of Mark). This book, which focuses on the miracles and actions of Jesus' life, is written for a non-Jewish (or *Gentile*) audience. The Gospel of Matthew, by comparison, is written to the Jews. Attributed to a tax collector who was one of Jesus' 12 apostles, it uses many scripture references to prove that Jesus is the Messiah. The Gospel of John is attributed to another of the apostles and contains more of Jesus' teachings than the other gospels. The author of the longest gospel, Luke, was an educated Greek doctor who served as a missionary. Luke also wrote the Acts of the Apostles, which provides an account of the early Christian Church.

According to Acts, after Jesus' ascension the apostles returned to Jerusalem, and were together in one place when the Holy Spirit descended upon them. Under the leadership of Peter, to whom Jesus had given a leading place among the apostles, they began to speak to others about Jesus Christ. First they spoke in the Temple, preaching to the Jews and performing miracles through the power of the Holy Spirit.

Jewish leaders were not happy that Jesus' followers had maintained their beliefs, which they considered to be blasphemous and heretical. The Sanhedrin ordered that the apostles be arrested, but Acts records that they were miraculously freed from prison. In one case, however, a Christian named Stephen was placed on trial before the Sanhedrin. When Stephen stated that Jesus was the Son of God, the angry Jews took him outside the Temple and murdered him.

This event set off a great wave of persecution against the Christians, forcing many to flee from Jerusalem. Leading this persecution was a devout Pharisee named Saul of Tarsus, who had been involved in the murder of Stephen. But while Saul was on the way to Damascus to attack the Christians there, he was struck blind and heard Jesus tell him to stop persecuting his followers.

Saul soon accepted Jesus' teachings. With his sight recovered and now known by the name Paul, he became one of the most important teachers and missionaries of early Christianity. Between 46 and 64 C.E. Paul traveled throughout the Roman world to spread the faith and establish churches. He wrote letters to the leaders of these churches, in which he set out the doctrine that would form the basis of Christianity.

Before Paul began his mission to the Gentiles, it was possible that Jesus' followers might eventually return to the greater Jewish community. They continued to worship God in the Temple and obeyed the Jewish law and scriptures along with Jesus' teachings. "The impression we get is that the Jerusalem Church was unstable, and had a tendency to drift back into Judaism completely," writes Paul Johnson in *A History of Christianity*. "Indeed, it was not really a separate Church at all, but part of the Jewish cult."

Paul did a great deal to change this. He had been born a Jew, but

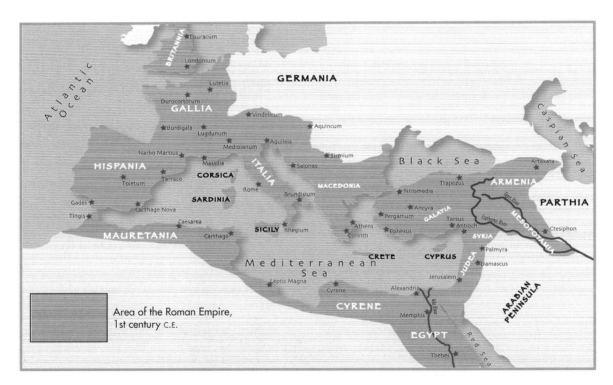

Area of the Roman Empire, 1st century C.E.

This map shows the Roman world during the time of Jesus and the development of the early Christian Church. The apostle Paul, a Roman citizen, was the first great missionary; he made four journeys through the Roman world teaching about Jesus. In letters to church leaders in Ephesus, Corinth, Rome, and other cities within the empire, Paul established Christian theology. These epistles, which date to 51 C.E., are the earliest writings in the New Testament.

he was also a Roman citizen and an admirer of Hellenistic culture. In his letters Paul explained that Jesus had come to replace Jewish law as the way to God. Salvation, he taught, came through faith in Jesus rather than in obedience to the law. All people, not just the Jews, could therefore be freed from their sin, and it became Paul's mission to spread this "good news" to the Gentile world. "[For Paul] the coming of Christ automatically ended the old Jewish law," writes Johnson. "For him the law had become a curse, for no man could fulfill its 613 commands and prohibitions completely; thus it made sinners of everyone."

Paul taught that anyone—regardless of racial or cultural background, gender, or social position—who accepted Jesus would in turn be chosen by God. This was a significant break from Judaism, which taught that Jews were God's people and had been chosen for greatness as long as they kept the law. Mainstream Judaism also could not accept the idea of Jesus as divine—this was inherently offensive to a religion based on the belief in one God. Most Jews did not convert, and some actively persecuted the Christians.

The rate of conversion was much greater among the Gentiles. Many of the Roman Empire's Greek-speaking people had been attracted to the monotheism and ethical code of Judaism, but had never accepted all of its rituals and dietary laws. Christianity offered an attractive alternative, and soon Christian communities were established in many cities throughout the empire.

The spread of Christianity attracted the attention of Rome. Like the Sanhedrin, Roman authorities saw Christianity as a threat to their control. The emperors believed in dealing quickly and efficiently with any movement that might cause political unrest. Christianity posed a potential threat because the movement was not confined to Judea. Imperial leaders construed Christians' refusal to follow the Roman custom and worship the emperors as gods as a sign that the Christians were disloyal to the empire and might be planning to revolt. Christianity's simple message of repentance and charity was also antithetical to the lavish and dissolute lifestyles of many Romans.

Over the next three centuries Christians would regularly be persecuted. During the rule of the emperor Nero (54–68 C.E.), Peter, Paul, and many of the apostles were executed. In 91 the emperor Domitian ordered attacks on Christians as well as Jews within the empire. During the rule of Marcus Aurelius, Christianity was made illegal in order to appease Rome's ancient gods after a rebellion by the Parthians. Other particularly severe persecutions of Christians occurred around 257 under Valerian, and from 303 to 313 under Diocletian.

The fact that Christians were so dedicated to their belief in Jesus that they were willing to die for the faith made others curious, however. Many people converted when they learned more about Christianity. "The blood of the martyrs is the seed of the church," wrote a Roman named Tertullian, who became a Christian in 197. But early in the fourth century Christianity's standing in Roman society would change dramatically, thanks to the influence of a powerful benefactor.

CONSTANTINE LEGITIMIZES CHRISTIANITY

When Diocletian became emperor of Rome in 284, the empire was facing serious military and economic troubles. He instituted a program of reforms that included separating the empire into eastern and western divisions. Diocletian took control of the eastern half of the empire and installed an associate to rule in the West. Eventually, he created positions for two lesser leaders (caesars) who served under the eastern and western emperors. This established a form of government called the Tetrarchy, in which four rulers (the two eastern and two western tetrarchs) had a great deal of power.

After Diocletian's rule ended in 305, a power struggle broke out among the empire's rulers. After a long struggle Constantine—the son of one of the western tetrarchs—eventually emerged as the sole ruler of the Roman Empire. Constantine attributed his success to divine intervention. Before an important battle in 312, Constantine saw a sign in the sky that he believed was sent by Jesus Christ, and he told his soldiers to place the symbol XP (the Greek letters *Chi* and *Rho*, the first two letters of *Christos*) on their shields. Winning the battle helped Constantine capture Rome and gave him control over the western half of the empire.

With gratitude Constantine, joined by the eastern tetrarch Licinius, in 313 issued the Edict of Milan, which declared that the Roman Empire would not discriminate against any religion and would cease persecution of Christians. This gave the religion greater legitimacy and led to explosive growth in the Christian population.

The struggle for control over the empire was not over, however. It was not until 324 that Constantine defeated his rival Licinius and became the sole ruler. Constantine soon set to work establishing an eastern capital, which was built on the site of an ancient Greek city

A Roman mosaic shows loaves of bread and fish, which commemorate one of Jesus' miracles. The fish was an early sign of Christianity, but as the religion spread throughout the Roman Empire, the cross eventually became the faith's main symbol.

called Byzantium. The city, renamed Constantinople, was closer than Rome to the most heavily populated parts of the empire, and in 330 it became the imperial capital.

Although Constantine did not immediately become a Christian, he remained interested in the religion. He was upset when he learned that Christian leaders disagreed on many theological questions. In 325 he invited several hundred of the major Christian leaders to a council at which the core beliefs of Christianity would be established once and for all.

Christian thinkers had begun to disagree over theological matters early in church history. There had been numerous variant movements within Christianity. One of the more famous of these was Gnosticism, a belief system influenced by Greek and Eastern thought in which the intellect was considered divine and the physical world evil. Gnostics rejected the Old Testament and many of

The Roman emperor Constantine (274–337 C.E.) was Christianity's most important patron. Under his protection persecution of Christians ended and the religion gained many new converts. Christianity ultimately became the official religion of the empire later in the fourth century.

the basic Christian teachings and were therefore condemned by mainstream Christian leaders.

The nature of Jesus was another question faced by early theologians. How could Christians reconcile worshipping Jesus as the divine Son of God when Jesus himself taught that humans should worship only one God? Was Jesus a man who became God through his suffering, or had he always been God? To explain this mystery, early church leaders developed the doctrine of the Trinity. This explained that the world and all things in it had been created by a single all-powerful God, but that He was composed of three parts: the Father, the Son, and the Holy Spirit. Each element of the Trinity was fully God, and therefore equally knowledgeable and powerful.

The doctrine of the Trinity was difficult for both Christians and non-Christians to understand. Some people believed that the Son and the Holy Spirit were less powerful than the Father because they had been created by God and did His bidding. In the early fourth century a Christian priest from Alexandria named Arius began to teach that Jesus, though divine, was a separate entity subservient to God. "[Arius saw] the coming forth of the divine Word as a service to the inferior created order," writes Henry Chadwick, former Regius Professor Emeritus of Divinity at Cambridge University. "He reasoned that the Lord who was physically born of Mary, grew in wisdom, suffered dereliction and death, must be less than the unbegotten, impassible, deathless Father."

This teaching, called Arianism, was accepted by some church leaders and rejected by others. As the doctrinal dispute threatened to split the church, Constantine encouraged Christian bishops to gather at Nicaea, a lakeside village in modern-day Turkey. At the Council of Nicaea, the church leaders rejected Arianism and adopted a creed that stated the basic beliefs of Christianity. With only minor modifications, this creed remains the basic Christian belief today:

We believe in one God, the Father, the Almighty, maker of heaven and earth, of all that is, seen and unseen.

We believe in one Lord, Jesus Christ, the only Son of God, eternally begotten of the Father, God from God, Light from Light, true God from true God, begotten, not made, one in Being with the Father.

Through him all things were made. For us men and for our salvation he came down from heaven: by the power of the Holy Spirit he was born of the Virgin Mary, and became man.

For our sake he was crucified under Pontius Pilate; he suffered, died, and was buried. On the third day he rose again in fulfillment of the Scriptures; he ascended into heaven and is seated at the right hand of the Father. He will come again in glory to judge the living and the dead, and his kingdom will have no end.

We believe in the Holy Spirit, the Lord, the giver of life, who proceeds from the Father and the Son. With the Father and the Son he is worshiped and glorified. He has spoken through the Prophets.

We believe in one holy catholic and apostolic Church. We acknowledge one baptism for the forgiveness of sins. We look for the resurrection of the dead, and the life of the world to come. Amen

There were other issues that divided Christianity. Churches in the eastern part of the empire observed rites and festivals that differed from the rites and festivals observed by churches in the western part, for example. The Council of Nicaea addressed these practices with the intention of standardizing them throughout the entire church.

When the council ended, Constantine thanked Christian leaders for agreeing on *dogma*. However, this did not end disputes over theological matters. Arianism, for example, spread to the Germanic tribes outside the empire, where it persisted as a variant Christian belief.

Constantine helped Christianity in many ways. He exempted the church from certain taxes and contributed to the construction of ornate basilicas in Rome, Jerusalem, and other places throughout the empire. He eventually outlawed pagan sacrifices and the worship of idols. His patronage encouraged many Romans to convert, as Constantine himself did just before he died in 337.

This Byzantine basilica mosaic shows Mary holding the infant Jesus while various saints kneel around them. Mary has a special place in Christianity, but beliefs about Jesus' mother vary among branches of the Christian faith. Roman Catholics and Orthodox Christians ask Mary to intercede on their behalf, but they do not believe Mary is divine and make a distinction between venerating Mary and worshipping her. Protestants reject veneration, fearing that it will take away from worship of God. Muslims and Jews both believe the practice of veneration crosses the line into idolatry.

But there was a downside to Constantine's influence on the church. His role in calling the Council of Nicaea and his interest in resolving other church disputes set a precedent for government involvement in religion. And his support for Christianity led many politically minded people to join the religion to further their career ambitions, rather than because they believed in its teachings.

Within the empire, Christianity gradually became the religion of choice for most people. It spread outside the empire as well, and by the middle of the fourth century it had been embraced by many of the Germanic tribes living on the fringes of Roman power.

EMPIRE AND CHURCH DIVIDED

Although Constantine had reunited the empire under his rule, after 395 the empire became permanently divided into eastern and western halves. There were many social differences between the two parts of the empire. Even the languages were different: Latin was spoken in Rome and the West, while Greek was the language of Constantinople and the East. But during the fourth and fifth centuries both sections of the empire were under growing pressure from outside forces. The "barbarian" Goths and Franks attacked the frontiers of the western empire, while to the east the empire had to deal with the growing strength of the Sassanid Persians. There were internal problems as well: regular civil wars over control of the empire and high taxes to support the large military. These factors kept the Roman Empire in a near-constant state of unrest.

Christianity officially became the state religion in 381, and other religions were outlawed. However, because in ancient Rome the rulers had also been *pontifex maximus*, or leader of the state religion, the emperors felt entitled to involve themselves in religious matters.

Over centuries, Christianity developed a sophisticated organization of church leaders. In the original churches established by the apostles, local leaders had been chosen to teach the believers, lead worship services, and induct new members into their community. By the third century, however, a hierarchy of church leaders was established to govern the Christian community more efficiently. A priest was appointed to lead each individual church. A bishop would oversee the activities of all of the churches in a particular city or region, to make sure priests were following the accepted church teachings. The bishops of Alexandria, Antioch, Jerusalem, Constantinople, and Rome were considered the most important, because they led the largest Christian communities or apostles had founded their churches. The accepted practice was for smaller communities faced with doctrinal questions they could not resolve to appeal to the closest major bishopric for a ruling on the issue.

The Roman church had a connection to two apostles: Peter and Paul had both been executed in Rome during Nero's rule. In the third century a church leader named Irenaeus claimed that Peter had been the first bishop of Rome, and that because of Peter's importance in the early church the Roman bishop (who eventually became known as the pope) should be considered the final authority for all decisions related to church doctrine. Because Rome was the most important bishopric in the western empire, its leadership was ultimately accepted by the churches of western Europe and North Africa.

The eastern Christian churches did not accept Rome's supremacy, however. They preferred to resolve disagreements over doctrine through consensus of church leaders. To achieve consensus, they called *ecumenical* councils of bishops. These first of these was the Council of Nicaea in 325; other important early councils were held at Constantinople (381), Ephesus (431), and Chalcedon (451). Although representatives of the Roman church participated at these councils, in which orthodox doctrine was established, they had no more influence than any other bishops.

By the fifth century the Byzantine Empire, as the eastern part of the empire came to be called, was the uncontested center of imperial power. The wealthiest provinces, such as Syria and Egypt, were located in the east, and the tax revenue they provided allowed Byzantine emperors to equip armies and protect their territories. The western emperors had fewer resources and so could not prevent invasions by Germanic tribes. Rome itself had fallen into decline, and the capital of the western empire was moved to Milan. As the western empire grew weaker, the popes gained greater power over both religious and secular life. When the Huns threatened Rome in 452, for example, it was Pope Leo, rather than the western emperor, who convinced their leader Attila not to attack the city. But even the church could not stop the ultimate collapse of the western empire in 476, when the last Roman emperor was deposed by invading German tribes.

The "fall" of the empire did not immediately cause an upheaval in European life. Rome itself was hardly damaged, and the lives of most people continued relatively unchanged. Many of the Germanic peoples had respected Roman laws and culture. Most tribal leaders had accepted Christianity—although of the variant form of Arianism—and they expected Christian bishops and priests to maintain order in their cities. "Hence the environment in which the Church now found itself was not, on the whole, hostile," writes Paul Johnson in *A History of Christianity*. "In the cities and the towns the bishops provided the natural elements of stability and local leadership. They were identified with conservation of the worthwhile past, continuity of administration, and the Roman tradition of peace and order."

Despite the collapse of the western empire, in the east Constantinople remained at the center of a brilliant civilization. The Byzantine Empire would survive the fall of Rome by nearly 1,000 years. But as differences in doctrine emerged, the two major

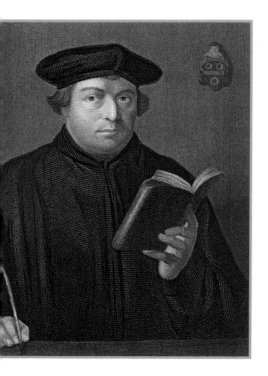

Martin Luther (1483–1546) was a leading figure in the Reformation, a 16th-century movement that split the western Christian Church. Luther and others originally protested corrupt practices of the Roman Catholic Church, but their requests for reform were scorned by church leaders. Ultimately, Luther and other reformers broke from the Roman Catholic Church completely; their new Christian sects became known as Protestant churches. The Protestants rejected the teachings of the popes, arguing that the Bible should be the only source of doctrine, and taught that people are saved only through belief in Jesus, rather than through any good things they might do during their lifetime.

branches of Christianity grew further apart. Although the eastern and western churches would remain in contact over the next 600 years, by 1054 Christianity officially separated into two churches: the Roman Catholic and Greek Orthodox, each of which believed its was the "true" church based on apostolic tradition and teachings.

Christianity would undergo other divisions in the centuries that followed. The most significant break occurred after the Reformation, which began in Europe during the 16th century as an effort to reform certain practices of the Roman Catholic Church and evolved into the establishment of new Christian churches, the Protestant denominations. But long before this, Christianity would find itself faced with a new challenge from outside: the rise of a new monotheistic faith that would turn the world upside-down in the seventh century.

An Egyptian man reads the Qur'an, the sacred scripture of Islam. Muslims believe the Qur'an contains the word of God, which He revealed to the prophet Muhammad.

The Emergence of Islam

By the beginning of the seventh century, Christianity had been the major religion of the Mediterranean world for more than 200 years. However, it had never spread widely into the Arabian Peninsula, which was sparsely populated by nomadic tribes. This desert region was far from the centers of Byzantine power.

The Arabian Peninsula was home to some Christian tribes, along with ascetics who wished to follow their faith alone in the desert. There were also tribes of people who practiced Judaism or the Persian religion Zoroastrianism. Most of the Arabs, though, were polytheists; they worshipped hundreds of different gods, and different tribes and clans often had their own deities. Three major goddesses that were most commonly worshipped were al-Uzza, al-Lat, and Manat. These were considered dependents of Allah ("the God"; the Arabic word *allah* simply means "god"), the creator god at the head of the Arab pantheon.

Around 400 C.E., a tribe of Arabs decided to settle down near the site of the ancient Kaaba shrine. This tribe, the Quraysh, established a city that would eventually be called Makka (Mecca). Because the region was not particularly good for agriculture, the 10 Quraysh clans engaged primarily in trade. They were skilled and successful traders. To encourage other tribes to visit Mecca, the Quraysh placed more than 350 different idols inside the Kaaba so that all of the Arabs' gods could be worshipped in the same place. The Kaaba became the site of a great annual pilgrimage of Arab tribes, and within two centuries Mecca was the commercial and spiritual center of western Arabia, a region known as the Hijaz.

Despite Mecca's central place in Arab religious life, the Quraysh were more interested in financial than in spiritual matters. Few cared for the poor and weak members of the community, although this had once been an integral value in Arab society. Women had practically no rights, and intertribal violence was common.

During the first half of the seventh century, a man named Muhammad emerged from this corrupt culture with a powerful message of spiritual reform and social justice. The new religion based on his teachings would emerge from the desert to sweep across much of the world in a remarkably short time.

DEVELOPMENT OF A NEW FAITH

Muhammad was born around 570 into a poor but respected Quraysh clan, the Hashim. As a young man, Muhammad worked on the caravans that traveled between Mecca and Damascus. After a wealthy Meccan widow named Khadija hired Muhammad as a business agent for her caravan and became impressed by his good qualities, the two married.

As a young man Muhammad worked on caravan routes between Mecca and Syria. This probably exposed him to a variety of cultural and religious practices, including Judaism and Christianity, which may have influenced the development of Islam.

As Muhammad grew older, he was widely respected as a wise and honest man. However, he was dissatisfied with the cruel society in which he lived, and each year he would retreat from Mecca to a nearby mountain, where he would spend time praying and meditating.

One night in the year 610, when Muhammad was about 40 years old, he was alone in the cave. The angel Gabriel appeared and told Muhammad that Allah was the only God, and that He wanted Muhammad to recite His message to the world. Muhammad was frightened and confused, but when he returned home his wife and cousin Ali comforted him. Over the next three years, as Muhammad received other revelations from God, he began to share the message with his family and friends in Mecca.

Over a period of several years, Muhammad's quiet preaching attracted a group of about 30 committed followers. These included his wife Khadija; his younger cousin Ali; his adopted son Zayd ibn Haritha; and a wealthy and respected merchant named Abu Bakr. Most of Muhammad's other followers were poor people and women. Muhammad's message appealed to them because it called for the establishment of a community that would not only revere the one true God, but also treat all of its members with fairness, equality, and respect.

Around 613 Muhammad began to proclaim his message to a wider audience. He told the people of Mecca that they should worship only Allah, that the idols in the Kaaba should be destroyed, and that the wealthy should share with the poor. Muhammad taught that all people must submit themselves to the will of Allah. The religion that developed around his teachings came to be called Islam, a name derived from the Arabic verb *aslama*, which means "submitted." Followers of Islam became known as Muslims, or "those who submit."

The wealthy Quraysh were not willing to submit to Muhammad's teachings: monotheism and social justice threatened their livelihoods. If people followed only Allah, the Quraysh leaders reasoned, they would stop traveling to Mecca to worship their other gods, and local merchants would lose a major source of revenue. Also, rich Meccans were not particularly interested in sharing their money with their less fortunate neighbors; nor were the aristocratic Meccans willing to share their high status with the lower classes. To stop the spread of Muhammad's message, the Quraysh passed laws prohibiting all business and social relations with Muslims. Muhammad's followers were persecuted. Some who could not earn a living starved to death, while others were beaten and killed for their beliefs. Muhammad was beaten and threatened with death. A group of Muslims left Mecca and fled to Africa, where they were sheltered in the Christian kingdom of Abyssinia.

In 621 representatives from Yathrib, an oasis city approximately 250 miles north of Mecca, invited Muhammad to come to their city. Two tribes there had been engaged in a violent rivalry for control of Yathrib, and they needed someone to help them resolve

their differences. In 622, in the face of continuing persecution, Muhammad and about 200 of his followers left Mecca and journeyed to Yathrib. This important event became known as the *Hijra* (the Arabic word means "migration" or to leave one's tribe).

In the Arab world of the seventh century, leaving Mecca was a major social adjustment. The tribe was the basis of Arab society,

The Islamic calendar starts with the *Hijra*, the migration of Muslims from Mecca to Yathrib. That event occurred in the year 622 C.E. according to the Western calendar. In Yathrib (now known as Medina), the original Islamic state was established and defended. Seen here is the Prophet's Mosque in Medina.

and members of a tribe were bound together by blood relationships and by moral and social obligations. By leaving the city
Muhammad and his followers had, in the eyes of the Meccans,
abandoned their tribal responsibilities. The Quraysh vowed to
destroy the Muslims for rejecting their own traditions and trying
to destroy them with the new message.

Muslims consider the Kaaba the
center of the world and believe it
was originally built by Adam as a
place of worship. After the Great
Flood, Abraham and Ishmael
rebuilt the structure, but over
the years it became filled with
pagan idols. After the Muslims
captured Mecca, Muhammad
and his cousin Ali cleansed the
Kaaba of idols and dedicated the
building to Allah.

When Muhammad arrived in Yathrib, he united the different tribes of the city under an agreement called the *wathiqat al-Madina*. This treaty bound the different tribes to cooperate in the mutual defense of the city and outlined a procedure for prosecuting crimes committed by a member of one tribe or community against a person of a different community. Under Muhammad's leadership, the Muslims flourished in Yathrib. The first mosque was built next to his house, and it became a center of religious and social activities. Many people of Yathrib accepted Muhammad's message, and Islamic ideas soon became the basis of the city's judicial and social systems. (After Muhammad's death, the city would become known as Madinat al-Nabi—"City of the Prophet"—or, more commonly in the West, Medina.)

In Islam the *umma*, or Muslim community, is the basis of all social relations. Members of the *umma* were expected to protect and defend one another regardless of their previous tribal affiliations. If any group within the *umma* was threatened, the rest of the *umma* was obliged to defend them. The concept of *umma* supplanted the traditional Arab notion of family and tribal obligations. Acceptance of this new social ideal was an important act of faith for the Muslims.

The need for solidarity became evident when warfare broke out between Mecca and Yathrib in 624. Muhammad's forces won an important victory at the Battle of Badr that year, but in 625 a Quraysh army routed the Muslims. In 627 the Meccans targeted Yathrib again, sending a large army to attack the city. The Muslims built defenses just in time to thwart the attack, and the Meccans were ultimately forced to withdraw in failure.

As the power of the Muslims in Yathrib grew, Muhammad began to make treaties with other Arab tribes outside the city. By 628 he felt that the Muslims were strong enough to undertake a pilgrimage to the Kaaba. He led about 2,000 Muslims toward Mecca, but a Meccan army stopped them. The Quraysh refused to let them continue the pilgrimage, but they did promise to allow the Muslims to visit the Kaaba the following year if Muhammad signed a peace agreement. He did, and in 629 the Muslims were permitted to worship Allah in the Kaaba.

Shortly after this, however, the Quraysh violated the nonaggression treaty, and in January 630 Muhammad led a 10,000-man army to Mecca. When the Muslims arrived, they found the Meccans dispirited, and the city was surrendered without a fight. Muhammad treated the defeated Meccans with mercy, which was more than he could have expected had the outcome been reversed. One of his first actions, though, was to enter the Kaaba and destroy the hundreds of idols located within. From this point forward the sacred building was to be dedicated to Allah alone. The destruction of the idols showed the people of Mecca how truly powerless their gods had been, and they were grateful for Muhammad's leniency. Soon most of the Meccans had become Muslims.

THE CORE ISLAMIC BELIEFS

All committed Muslims share certain beliefs and practices. The most important obligations of the religion are known as the five pillars of Islam. These include the profession of faith (*shahada*), daily prayer (*salat*), almsgiving (*zakat*), fasting during the month of Ramadan (*sawm*), and the pilgrimage to Mecca (*hajj*).

The profession of faith in God is a prerequisite for anyone who wishes to join the Muslim community. It involves a simple statement: "There is no god but Allah, and Muhammad is His messenger."

Muslims reaffirm their faith during each of their five prescribed daily prayers. These are recited at dawn, noon, mid-afternoon, sunset, and evening. At one time Muhammad and his followers in Yathrib faced Jerusalem while praying, but Muhammad later declared that God had told him that the faithful should face the Kaaba when praying. Therefore, most mosques have niches or markings that indicate the direction of Mecca. Although Muslims can perform most of the prayers either by themselves or with oth-

This Asian Muslim is kneeling in prayer, one of the five major requirements of Islam. Muslims are required to say five prayers at different times of each day.

ers, they are required to worship together at noon on Fridays.

The third pillar of Islam is the obligation of Muslims to help the poor, which is stressed throughout the Qur'an. There are two forms of charitable giving: a mandatory tax (*zakat*) and voluntary almsgiving (*sadaqa*).

The fourth pillar of Islam is the command to fast during Ramadan, one of the 12 months of the Islamic lunar calendar. Ramadan is considered a sacred month because it was during this month that Muhammad received his first revelations. During Ramadan, Muslims must refrain from eating, drinking, and certain other physical pleasures from dawn to sunset each day. The purpose of the fast is to practice physical and spiritual discipline, to serve as a reminder of the trials of the poor, and to build a sense of solidarity among all Muslims. At the end of Ramadan, Muslims celebrate with a three-day holiday of breaking the fast that is known as Eid al-Fitr.

The fifth pillar of Islam calls for Muslims to make a pilgrimage to Mecca at least once during their lifetime, provided they are physically and financially able to do so. This pilgrimage, known as the hajj, is a powerful spiritual experience for many Muslims. Muslims from all walks of life make the journey to Mecca. The spiritual objective of the pilgrimage is to set aside worldly concerns and to commune with God. So all pilgrims—regardless of their station in the outside world—are to be considered equals when they are in Mecca.

Islam is more than a religion; it is a way of life, and submission to God involves following His regulations concerning everyday life, commerce, and social relations. The five pillars are not prescribed in the Qur'an, but are based on Muhammad's traditions. The Qur'an does not contain much information about specific religious or social practices. For example, the Qur'an says that Muslims should pray, but it does not explain the manner in which they should pray. As a result, through centuries of study and discussion Muslims developed a catalog of restrictions and obligations that became known as *Sharia*. This body of rules, sometimes called Islamic law, is observed by devout Muslims today.

EARLY GROWTH OF THE ISLAMIC STATE

By the time Muhammad died in 632, most of the tribes on the Arabian Peninsula had submitted to Islam. For the first time in history the Arabs were united politically and religiously. They soon began to take control of neighboring regions. Within 100 years the Arab Islamic state had conquered the Persian Empire. It also conquered Syria, Egypt, and other areas of Africa and the eastern Mediterranean that had been ruled by the Byzantine

Empire. Islam even spread into western Europe: in 711 Arab-Berber Moors from North Africa invaded the Iberian Peninsula.

As the Arab armies conquered new lands, they offered the defeated people an opportunity to convert to Islam. This was supposed to be a free decision because the Qur'an forbids forcible conversion. Some people found Islam an attractive alternative to their old beliefs. This was particularly true of the Monophysites of Syria and Egypt, who appreciated Islam's message that Allah was the only God and that He did not have children or a Trinitarian nature. Others converted for a more worldly reason, recognizing that as Muslims they would have greater rights in the Islamic state.

Jews and Christians were permitted to keep their religions, if they wished. Muhammad had taught that because the Jews and Christians had received divine messages through their scriptures, which teach monotheism, they should be considered *ahl al-kitab* (people of the book), and therefore be protected (*dhimmi*). However, those who did not convert had to swear allegiance to the Islamic state and pay a special tax. The Islam expert Bernard Lewis explains:

> In early days the *dhimmis* constituted the overwhelming majority of the inhabitants of all the Muslim lands except the Arabian peninsula. Provided that they were followers of a recognized and tolerated religion, such as Judaism or Christianity, they were not subject—apart from occasional and exceptional outbursts of fanaticism—to any pressure to adopt Islam, and indeed in earlier times were sometimes discouraged from taking a step which would have decreased the revenues and increased the expenditure of the state. Despite this, however, the movement of conversion continued steadily and, at a date which it is impossible to determine precisely, and which varied from place to place, the majority of the population in the countries of the Middle East and North Africa came to be Muslim, while the earlier religions declined and in some areas disappeared. In the eastern lands important Christian minorities survived, especially in Egypt, Palestine, Syria, and to a lesser extent in Iraq, where rather smaller Jewish minorities also remained. In the Arab West, in North Africa, Christianity died out, though Judaism survived in some strength. . . .

Throughout, Jews and Christians continued to play an important part in the government of the Islamic empires and particularly in the administrative services of the state.

The Islamic state claimed its legitimacy from God, but it had to be administered by human beings. Though considered God's most important messenger, Muhammad—the *umma's* first leader—was never regarded as divine. Upon his death, the Muslim community needed to select another person to succeed the Prophet as head of the *umma*. The difficult choice was whether the caliph (from the Arabic word *khalifa*, meaning "successor") should be chosen on the basis of his family relationship to Muhammad, or on the basis of his wisdom and piety. Ultimately, leaders of the community decided to take the latter path. They chose Abu Bakr, a close confidant of Muhammad and an early convert, as the first caliph, passing over Muhammad's cousin and son-in-law, Ali.

Abu Bakr ruled for two years, until his death in 634. He was followed by Umar (634–644), Uthman (644–656), and Ali (656–661). These four are known as the *rashidun*, or "rightly guided caliphs." They had all known Muhammad personally and had worked directly with him to build the Islamic community. Their approximately 30 years of rule were marked by great accomplishments, including the compilation of the Qur'an and a remarkable period of expansion.

When Ali was assassinated in 661, power over the Islamic state passed into the hands of the Umayyad clan. Muslims had chosen the first four caliphs, but the Umayyad caliph Muawiya named his son Yazid as his successor, establishing a dynasty that would last until 750.

The power struggle between Ali and Muawiya, Ali's assassination, and the murder of Ali's son Hussein in 680 by the Umayyads caused a major rift in the Muslim community. The larger group of Muslims continued to follow the Umayyad caliphs; they became known as Sunni Muslims. A smaller group, which had revered Ali and Hussein, argued that the Umayyad caliphs were not legitimate and instead supported the descendants of Ali. They became known as the Shiites. Although Shiites and Sunnis agreed on the major points of Islamic doctrine, the Shiites developed additional traditions and beliefs that differed from those of the mainstream Sunnis.

THE DEVELOPMENT OF ISLAMIC LAW

Sunni Muslims, who make up about 85 percent of the worldwide Muslim population today, believe they are obeying the path laid out by Muhammad through his teachings and his exemplary life. The revelations received by Muhammad were recorded in the

A book of Islamic legal opinions, dating from the year 808, is open on a shelf in the Khalidi Library, Jerusalem. Islamic jurists used legal decisions and rulings to establish a comprehensive code of conduct, including laws and punishments for breaking those laws. This code is known as *Sharia*, from an Arabic word meaning "the way."

Qur'an, while stories about Muhammad and his teachings on religious and nonreligious matters were preserved separately. These stories were not written down at first; instead Muhammad's companions remembered them and told them to others. Muhammad's words and deeds and those of the early Muslims are known collectively as the *Sunna*, an Arabic word that means "the path." Narrations about the Sunna are called "Hadith." Hadith is considered the second source of Islamic law—the first being the Qur'an.

Many of the companions were still alive during the rule of the rightly guided caliphs, and they could be counted on to make religious decisions based on their experiences with Muhammad. By the time of Ali's death, however, most of the companions were also dead, and a new generation of Muslims was responsible for transmitting the Hadith. Eventually, unreliable Hadith began to be added to the oral tradition. Some of these were benign, intending only to further glorify Muhammad's life, but others were the product of attempts to justify people's own behavior or views, when they were at odds with Islamic teachings.

The rapid growth of Islam caused additional problems. Expansion into new lands meant that the Islamic world encompassed a bewildering array of tribal and cultural practices. For the first time, many Arabs were exposed to the philosophical thought of the ancient Greeks, Romans, and Persians. Some Muslims, influenced by these older cultures, attempted to introduce new doctrines into Islam.

As Jews and Christians had previously discovered, to protect the religion meant that an organized structure of religious law and ritual had to be created, so that new converts could be clear on what kinds of actions were acceptable and what kinds were not. During the eighth century, Muslim jurists and theologians focused on clarifying Islam's dogmatic and theological beliefs and codifying these into a body of rules that would guide the *umma*. (Muslim scholars, jurists, and theologians who could interpret scripture and formulate dogma became known collectively as the *ulama*.)

During the eighth century, practices were developed to verify the authenticity of the Hadith. Between 815 and 912, experts sifted through thousands of stories, eliminating those that were obviously false and authenticating or discarding those that remained. Ultimately, six collections of Hadith were created. Two collections in particular are considered the most worthwhile: those of Muhammad ibn Ismail al-Bukhari and of Muslim ibn al-Hajjaj.

Through study of the Qur'an and the authentic Hadith, the *ulama* ultimately developed an inventory of acceptable and restricted behaviors and actions. This is known as *Sharia* (Arabic for "way") and is considered an all-embracing system that should govern every aspect of Islamic life.

To create this body of law, the *ulama* used two important principles. One was reasoning by analogy (*qiyas*), by which Muslim jurists could take restrictions or permissions that are clearly defined in the Qur'an or Hadith and apply them to comparable situations. For example, the Qur'an prohibits the consumption of wine, so jurists determined that Muslims could not drink any alcoholic beverages. The other principle used in the creation of law was the consensus of the community (*ijma*). If an issue arose that was not covered in the Qur'an or the Hadith, the leading scholars of the Muslim community could decide how best to proceed. These important principles provided flexibility for the Muslims to address the variety of problems they would encounter in their newly conquered territories, as long as they acted according to the basic tenets of the Qur'an. The process of using *qiyas* and *ijma* to interpret the holy law is called *ijtihad*.

Islamic jurists developed numerous schools of legal thought during the eighth and ninth centuries; four of these remain accepted today. Each school is named for the jurist on whose teaching it is based: Abd Allah Malik ibn Anas (Maliki school), An Numan ibn Thabit Abu Hanifa (Hanafi school), Muhammad ibn Idris al-Shafii (Shafii school), and Ahmad ibn Muhammad ibn Hanbal (Hanbali school). These schools share the same general rules of faith, but

The crescent symbol is often seen atop mosques; it is also used on the flags of some Muslim countries. However, Islam has no official symbol because of the religion's prohibition against representing God in art or any other physical form. The Ottoman Turks were the first to use the crescent symbol, and because of their long tenure ruling most of the world's Muslim population, the symbol came to be identified with Islam.

because each considered different Hadith to be most important, they differ slightly on the specifics of Islamic practice and on certain philosophical and theological issues.

The legal schools initially developed in such a way that they could adapt to accommodate new situations. However, by the 11th century many Muslims believed all of the important questions related to their faith had been answered. This led to a general agreement prohibiting significant changes to the law, which became known as "closing the gates of *ijtihad*."

GROWTH OF THE ISLAMIC EMPIRE

During the first decades of rule by the Umayyad caliphs, the Islamic world was divided by civil wars as various factions fought for power. Muhammad and the first four caliphs had ruled from Medina, and had lived simply as an example to other Muslims. The Umayyads, by contrast, moved the capital of the Islamic state to Damascus, where their strength was based, and craved wealth and the splendor of royalty. Their lavish excesses angered pious Muslims, and Umayyad caliphs often had to put down revolts in order to keep their power.

The Umayyads were able to establish a well-organized bureaucracy so that their far-flung territories could be efficiently administered. This strengthened the Islamic state and prepared it for further growth. As a result, a second great period of

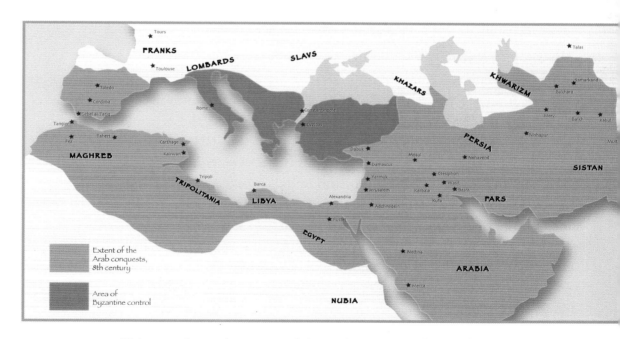

This map shows the extent of the Arab conquests during the first century after Muhammad's death. The Muslims had destroyed the Sassanid Empire in Persia, conquered former Byzantine territories in North Africa and the eastern Mediterranean, and invaded western Europe.

Islamic expansion began in 700. By 711 Muslim armies from North Africa had invaded western Europe. They moved north through the Iberian Peninsula until 732, when their advance was halted at the Battle of Poitiers (also known as the Battle of Tours). The Arabs also sent their armies into Asia and besieged Constantinople between 717 and 718. Though they seized additional territory, they were unable to destroy the Byzantine Empire.

During this period Islam did not spread only through conquest; the number of believers also continued to grow through conversion by more peaceful means. Traders or missionaries, rather than soldiers, first exposed many people to the tenets of Islam, particularly in Asia.

The exchange of ideas through contact with other cultures helped Islam to develop and, in many ways, shaped the direction of the Islamic state. The Umayyad caliphs encouraged the free exchange of ideas, and this tolerance, combined with military might, contributed to an Islamic culture in which intellectual pursuits could flourish.

The Umayyad caliphs were ultimately overthrown in a civil war, and a new family, the Abbasids, took power over the Islamic state in 750. During the five centuries in which they reigned, the process of intellectual development continued, and the Islamic state reached its greatest glory. At the same time the great jurists were codifying the laws of Islam, Muslim scholars were establishing themselves in other areas: mathematics, natural sciences, medicine, fine arts, architecture, philosophy, astronomy, and geography. The Muslims were able to take the work of great thinkers and scientists of the ancient world, such as Plato and Aristotle, and build upon them. Thus, while Christian Europe stagnated in its "dark ages," the Islamic world became the brilliant center of knowledge and learning.

With the Arab armies victorious nearly everywhere they turned, at one point in the eighth century it seemed as if the entire world might fall under Islamic control. Some Muslims believed the

Arabs' rapid conquests were proof that their religion was God's final plan for all humankind. But many Christians and Jews were not willing to give up their own monotheistic beliefs, and contact between the three monotheistic faiths would often lead to conflict between the spiritual descendants of Abraham.

This woodcut from a German pamphlet published in 1510 shows Jews desecrating a piece of the consecrated bread considered sacred by Christians. At the left, a man is about to stab the bread with a hunting knife. Inflammatory publications like this often led to violent attacks on Jewish populations in Europe.

A Legacy of Oppression

For most of the past 2,000 years, Jews have been minority populations in lands ruled by others—often Christians or Muslims. As a result, Jews have generally faced more oppression and discrimination than followers of the other faiths. In the early history of Christianity, Jews were among the persecutors, accusing the Jewish followers of Jesus of blasphemy. Christianity originally developed as a sect within Judaism and did not become a separate religion until about 85 C.E., when Jewish Christians were expelled from the synagogues.

By the end of the third century, communities of both Christians and Jews coexisted in nearly every Roman province. Christians were more likely than Jews to be persecuted by the state, but this changed under Constantine and his successors. As Christianity became the imperial religion, many other religions were destroyed. Judaism, however, was permitted to persist. "The accommodation of the Jews in western Christian society derives largely from the fact that Judaism could be located on a lower rung of the hierarchy of revelation which led to Christianity," explains Jeremy Johns, a lecturer at Oxford University.

Although the Edict of Milan was a policy of tolerance toward all religions within the empire, Jews began to be widely treated as second-class citizens during the rule of Constantine's son Constantius II (337–361). Taxes on Jews were increased, and Jews lost some of the rights of other Roman citizens. Jews could not marry Christians, they could not participate in the government, and they were no longer permitted to *proselytize*. The emperor Theodosius ultimately outlawed the practice of Judaism, along with all pagan religions, in 391.

Mistreatment of Jews was not confined to the government. Jews had once persecuted the Christian Church; now it was the church's turn. "During the third and fourth centuries various Church Fathers and councils put together the basic themes of what Jules Isaac has called 'The teaching of contempt,'" writes Daniel Jeremy Silver in *A History of Judaism*. "Judaism was depicted as a narrow legalism and scandalous superstition; Jews were *deicides*, and the destruction of the Temple was proof of God's anger against them. To keep Jews a people apart and deprived was to fulfill God's will; to bring them to the light of the true faith was an act of kindness, even if conversion must be done forcibly."

The claim that Jews were guilty of deicide—the murder of God—came from a reference in the Gospel of Matthew. After Jesus is arrested, he is tortured and questioned by Pontius Pilate, the Roman ruler of Jerusalem. Pilate tells a crowd of Jews that he wants to set Jesus free, but they instead clamor for his execution. Matthew writes: "When Pilate saw that he was getting nowhere, but that instead an uproar was starting, he took water and washed his hands in front of the crowd. 'I am innocent of this man's blood,' he said. 'It is your responsibility.' All the people answered, 'Let his blood be on us and on our children' " (Matthew 27: 24–25). This passage was used to justify attacks on Jews as punishment for their supposed complicity in the crucifixion. After Christian priests and monks preached inflammatory sermons on these verses, angry mobs would leave the churches to destroy local synagogues and attack Jewish communities. There are reports of such attacks as early as the 4th century, and as recently as the 20th.

The refusal of Jews to accept Jesus as divine, along with their use

Although most Christians have rejected the charge that Jews are guilty of deicide, even in the 21st century many Jews fear this unfair accusation will be resurrected. In 2004 Jewish groups in the United States protested outside screenings of the movie *The Passion of the Christ*, claiming that the film portrays Jews as responsible for Jesus' crucifixion.

of the Hebrew language, traditional dress, dietary restrictions, and practices of worship, made them different from other Europeans. Jews were eventually forced to live together in areas called ghettos, and they were regularly subjected to harassment in western Europe. During the 13th century the Roman Catholic Church established the Inquisition, the goal of which was to root out heresy. Thousands of Jews who refused to give up their beliefs were tortured and put to death.

"The popular dislike for Jews . . . creates a soil fertile for the Jew-baiting of the Medieval Church, and leads to such atrocities as the Russian *pogroms*, the York Massacre in England, and the slaughter of Jews during the Crusades in France and Germany,"

In the 19th and 20th centuries, Jewish communities in eastern Europe came under attack. Beginning in the 1880s, a series of pogroms left many Jews dead or homeless. This photograph, taken around 1909, shows a group of murdered Jews laid out on a Russian street.

explain Shlomo Shoham and Daniel Levine in a 1995 article in the *Journal of Criminal Justice and Popular Culture*. "The rise of nationalism, the failure of Jews to integrate fully, and the rise of their own national consciousness fed latent anti-Semitism in the West, and so gave rise to the idea that Jews are a different race, genetically incapable of integration, and requiring more drastic measures such as disenfranchisement, expulsion, and a host of other discriminatory policies."

Some Jews in Germany hoped that the 16th-century movement to reform the western church, which was led by Martin Luther, John Calvin, and others, would eliminate anti-Jewish attitudes. Luther, who had studied Judaism and written admiringly about the religion in 1523, apparently hoped that though Jews had historically rejected Christianity, they would flock to his new reformed (or Protestant) church. When German Jews stubbornly clung to their religion, Luther launched vitriolic attacks, calling them a "damned, rejected race" in his pamphlet *On the Jews and Their Lies* (1546). Writings like this led to new waves of persecution and hatred.

It was not just the Roman Christians who persecuted the Jews. Jews living in Russia, where the Greek Orthodox Church had great influence, were subject to attacks almost as often as were Jews in the West. The greatest danger often occurred on Good Friday, the day that commemorated the crucifixion, as Christian churchgoers were often whipped into a fury against their Jewish neighbors. Jews had to lock themselves in their homes or hide with their possessions to avoid rampaging mobs. The violence against Jews in Russia culminated with a series of pogroms from the 1880s through the 1910s. As a result of the violence, many Jews left eastern Europe. Most came to the United States, where the Jewish American population increased from less than 300,000 in 1880 to more than 4.5 million by 1930. Other Jews—inspired by a movement called Zionism, which aimed to reestablish a Jewish state in the land where the Israelite kingdoms had once flourished—tried to move to Palestine.

JEWS IN MUSLIM LANDS

The Jews who wished to settle in Palestine had to get the permission of the Muslim Ottoman Empire. The Ottoman Turks had emerged as the major power in the Islamic world after the decline of the Mongol Empire in the 14th century. They ultimately captured Constantinople and destroyed the Byzantine Empire in 1453. Like previous Muslim empires, the Ottomans permitted Jews and Christians to keep their religions.

Jews could live peacefully in religious communities, called *millets*, within the empire as long as they maintained allegiance to the Ottoman sultan. (There were Greek Christian *millets* in the Ottoman Empire as well.) Life was not perfect for members of these minority religious groups, who were under all of the traditional obligations of *dhimmi* and were occasionally subject to violence from the Muslims in power. In general, though, Jews were safer with the Muslims than they were in Christian Europe.

The history of interaction between Muslims and Jews has also been long, violent, and filled with oppression. Muhammad came into contact with Arab Jewish tribes, as well as with Jews in Syria, even before receiving his first revelation from God. While the Muslims were establishing their community in Medina after the *Hijra*, they shared the town with Jewish tribes who signed the *wathiqat al-Madina* treaty for defense of the city. The Jews did not accept Muhammad as a prophet, and in turn Muhammad argued that Jews had deviated from true worship of God.

After Muhammad's army was badly beaten by the Quraysh in 625, the Muslims forced one of the Jewish tribes of Yathrib, the Banu Qaynuqa' to leave the city because this tribe had violated the agreement by not coming to the aid of the Muslims. During the siege of Yathrib in 627, another Jewish tribe in the city, the Banu Qurayza, secretly conspired to let the Meccans into Yathrib through the gate they guarded. This plot was unsuccessful, and after the Meccan army withdrew, Muhammad and the Muslims attacked the Banu Qurayza, who eventually surrendered.

According to tradition, their punishment—in which all the men of the tribe were killed—was taken from the Torah: "If they refuse to make peace and they engage you in battle, lay siege to that city. When the Lord your God delivers it into your hand, put to the sword all the men in it. As for the women and children, the livestock and everything else in the city, you may take these as plunder for yourselves" (Deuteronomy 20: 12–14).

Muhammad established the system under which Jews could live as *dhimmi* within lands conquered by the Arabs. Although Jews in Muslim lands had to pay extra taxes and had fewer privileges than Muslims, they also were less likely to face the kind of persecution that Jews endured in the West. Jews were permitted to hold positions in the government, operate businesses, and own property.

An example of a state in which Jews and Christians thrived under Muslim government was the kingdom of al-Andalus in western Europe. The Muslim Moors from North Africa had invaded the Iberian Peninsula in the early eighth century. Some Christians and Jews fled the territory in the face of the Muslim invasion, while others remained and converted to Islam. Still others stayed as *dhimmi*, and their population was supplemented by the arrival of Jews and Christians emigrating from other lands conquered by Muslims.

At a time when the civilization of Christian Europe had fallen into its "dark ages," al-Andalus would become the most important Western center of learning. In cities like Córdoba, Toledo, Granada, and Seville, Christians, Jews, and Muslims lived and worked together in relative peace, exchanging the accumulated knowledge of their cultures. This period, known as the *convivencia*, allowed the growth and development of many areas of learning that had stagnated in Europe after the fall of the Roman Empire. These included philosophy, mathematics, science, art and literature, and architecture.

"Commercially and economically speaking, Muslims, Jews and Christians were all important, and in many instances, codependent contributors to the prosperity of medieval Spain," notes F. E. Peters, a professor at New York University who has written extensively on the three major monotheistic faiths. "Each community fed off the other's rich linguistic and literary heritage and poetic visions: Hebrew, Arabic and the beginnings of Romance lyric all came forth from that rich cultural mix."

Life was not completely harmonious; in 1066, for example, Muslims massacred Jews in Granada because they disliked a certain Jewish government official. However, tolerance, rather than violence, was the norm for the Muslims in Spain. Islamic tolerance

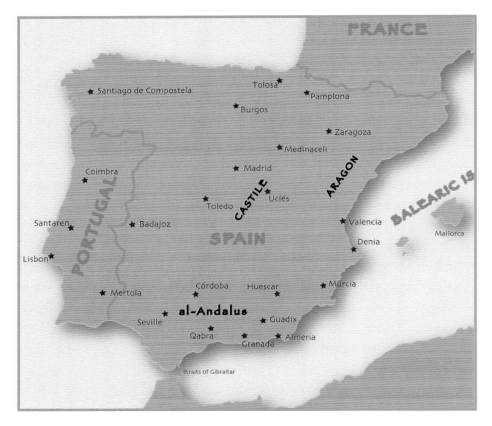

The Muslims who invaded the Iberian Peninsula in the eighth century established the kingdom of al-Andalus in the southern part of what today is the country of Spain. Al-Andalus was the center of knowledge in western Europe, and Jews, Christians, and Muslims lived and worked together there in relative harmony.

even induced some Jews to convert. As Bernard Martin writes in *A History of Judaism*:

> The Jews of medieval Europe seem to have resisted Christian influence more than Moslem. This difference in attitude is no doubt to be accounted for mainly by the difference in treatment they received from adherents of the two faiths. While the oppression suffered by the Jews at the hands of Moslem fanatics was neither slight nor sporadic, it cannot be compared to the massive and sustained persecutions visited on them by Christian zealots, particularly in the era of the Crusades and the centuries that followed. It must also be noted that the theological and ritual differences dividing Judaism from Christianity are far more substantial than those distinguishing it from Islam. . . . There was nothing in [Islam] like the deicide charge, with its potential for murderous explosion, or the compulsion to engage in systematic inculcation of contempt for Jews.

This would remain the case for centuries. The Ottoman Turks, for example, invited Jews to live within their empire; many accepted and moved east, where they would be safer than in the western Christian world.

A WARMING RELATIONSHIP

The relationship between Judaism and Christianity became more tolerant in the 20th century. Many Christians were shocked to learn the extent of the pogroms against Russian Jews during the 1930s, in which millions were murdered and buried in mass graves. Westerners were even more horrified by the Holocaust in Nazi Germany, in which nearly 6 million Jews were systematically killed.

Partially in response to these atrocities, Christianity began to change its positions. At the groundbreaking Second Vatican Council (1962–65), the Roman Catholic Church declared that Jews could not be held accountable for Jesus' death, that persecution and anti-Semitism were un-Christian, and that no one should be forced to convert or change his or her religious views. The Catholic Church would later apologize for not doing enough to stop the Holocaust while it was occurring.

Protestant Christian churches have followed the Catholic Church's lead. Presbyterian Church (USA), an organization that oversees Presbyterian churches in the United States, issued a statement that says in part, "We affirm that the church, elected in Jesus Christ, has been engrafted into the people of God established by the covenant with Abraham, Isaac and Jacob. Therefore, Christians have not replaced Jews." A statement on the issue by the United Church of Christ says, "We pray for divine grace that

The nave of St. Peter's Basilica in Rome is filled with 2,300 churchmen from all over the world, who have gathered for the final session of the three-year-long Second Vatican Council in December 1965. One statement issued by the council, *Nostra Aetate*, invalidated the charge of deicide against Jews. The statement reads in part, "In her rejection of every persecution against any man, the Church, mindful of the patrimony she shares with the Jews and moved not by political reasons but by the Gospel's spiritual love, decries hatred, persecutions, displays of anti-Semitism, directed against Jews at any time and by anyone." In *Nostra Aetate* the Roman Catholic Church also acknowledged that Muslims believe in the same God as Christians: "They adore one God, living and enduring, merciful and all-powerful, Maker of heaven and earth and Speaker to men. They strive to submit wholeheartedly even to His inscrutable decrees, just as did Abraham, with whom the Islamic faith is pleased to associate itself."

will enable us, more firmly than ever before, to turn from this path of rejection and persecution to affirm that Judaism has not been superseded by Christianity; that Christianity is not to be understood as the successor religion to Judaism; God's covenant with the Jews has not been abrogated. God has not rejected the Jewish people; God is faithful in keeping covenant."

As Christians acknowledge their religion's history of anti-Jewish bias, they become more interested in learning about Jewish culture, to better understand the context in which events of the Old and New Testaments are rooted. Jews have also attempted to learn more about Christianity and its teachings. A small number of Jewish people, sometimes known as Messianic Jews, have come to accept Jesus as the Messiah while retaining their Jewish heritage.

One issue Western Christians and Jews generally agree on—although many Arab and Eastern Orthodox Christians hold a differing point of view—is the right of the state of Israel to exist. Israel was formed after World War II in Palestine, where a Jewish state had existed in ancient times. Some evangelical Christians believe that a Jewish state is necessary to fulfill prophecies of Jesus' Second Coming. Others simply identify Israel with the ancient land where God spoke to Abraham, David ruled a mighty kingdom, and Jesus and his disciples walked.

POLITICAL DIVISIONS

Although in some respects the state of Israel has unified Jews and Christians in the West, the issue has divided Muslims and Jews. Although the Ottoman Turks permitted some Jews to immigrate to Palestine during the late 19th and early 20th centuries, the settlers were not always welcomed by Arabs, who had lived there for generations. Tension increased when Great Britain took control of Palestine after World War I. As Jewish communities grew during the 1920s and 1930s, they at times found themselves in conflict with their Arab neighbors.

After the Holocaust, many Europeans and Americans wanted to

establish a separate state for Jews. In 1947 the newly formed
United Nations presented a plan to divide Palestine into Jewish
and Arab Palestinian states. Because of Jerusalem's spiritual
importance to Jews, Christians, and Muslims alike, the city was to
be administered by the U.N. and open to all faiths. The U.N. plan
was never implemented, however. When Britain pulled out of
Palestine in May 1948, Jewish leaders declared the independent
state of Israel, and five neighboring Arab countries immediately
attacked.

By 1949, when the fighting ended, Israel had not only survived,
but actually expanded its territory beyond what was to have been
allotted it under the U.N. partition plan. The Palestinian Arabs, by
contrast, were left with no land of their own. Israel had taken part
of the territory, including part of Jerusalem; Jordan controlled the
Old City and East Jerusalem, along with the territory known as
the West Bank; and Egypt held the Gaza Strip.

Fighting continued between Israel and the Arabs over the next
two decades. In June 1967, Israel launched a preemptive strike
against Egypt, Syria, and Jordan. During the brief war, Israel captured the West Bank and Gaza Strip territories and took control
over all of Jerusalem.

Since 1967, Muslims throughout the world have denounced
Israel's occupation of Jerusalem and the other Arab territories.
Control over Jerusalem has been a key issue in Israeli-Palestinian
violence, particularly since September 2000.

The violence in Palestine is motivated more by nationalism than
religion, as Arab Palestinians believe their claim to the land to be
more valid than Israel's. But there is an important religious com-
ponent to the dispute because of the reverence in which Muslims
hold Jerusalem, which is considered Islam's third-holiest city.

Jerusalem's significance to Muslims stems from an event
described in the Qur'an and Hadith. One night, Muhammad is
awakened by angels and led to the Kaaba. From there, a winged,
horse-like creature called al-Buraq flies the Prophet to Jerusalem.
Landing on the ruins of the ancient Jewish Temple, Muhammad

An Israeli soldier guards a checkpoint between Bethlehem and Jerusalem, November 2003. The Palestinians on the other side are hoping to enter Jerusalem to pray on the final Friday of Ramadan.

dismounts from al-Buraq and prays. Then al-Buraq carries the Prophet to heaven, where Muhammad receives the command to pray five times a day and meets with Abraham, Moses, Jesus, and other messengers of God. Because of this, Muslims have long considered Jerusalem a holy city, and at one time early in Muslim history Muhammad told his followers to face Jerusalem, rather than Mecca, when they prayed.

The most important Islamic shrine in Jerusalem is al-Masjid al-Aqsa (the Aqsa Mosque), which includes the famous Dome of the Rock. This was built over the rock on which Muslims believe Muhammad stood to mount al-Buraq for his ascent to heaven. But this is also sacred ground for Jews: the Temple Mount, where the ancient Jewish Temple stood.

In part because neither side is willing to give up control of its spiritual history in Jerusalem, peace negotiations between Israel and the Palestinians have never succeeded. The ongoing violence in Israel has angered both Muslims and Jews around the world, straining relations between the two groups.

President George W. Bush, surrounded by American Islamic leaders, speaks out against rising anti-Muslim sentiment in the United States a week after the September 11, 2001, terrorist attacks.

Mistrust and Violence

Muhammad taught his followers that Islam was the true religion—the one God had given to Abraham. Muslims therefore believe that Islam *preceded* Judaism and Christianity. After Abraham's death, Muhammad said, God's commandments were misunderstood or forgotten, so God sent messengers, such as Moses and Jesus, to guide humanity back to the correct path. Although these prophets had brought important messages, their followers had distorted their teachings. Muslims believe Muhammad was God's final messenger, and therefore the revelations given to him and recorded in the Qur'an supersede the earlier messages of Moses and Jesus.

As Islam spread rapidly during the seventh and eighth

centuries, devout Christians became disturbed at the teachings of this new faith. They considered the Muslims' claims, especially their rejection of Jesus' divinity, to be heretical. Latin Christian writers quickly attacked Islam as a dangerous mutation of monotheism and encouraged Christians to remain firm in their faith. Eastern Christians, many of whom lived in cities seized in the early Arab conquests, also argued against Islam. One of the most famous *apologists* was a Syrian known as John of Damascus, who around the middle of the eighth century held a high government position in the Islamic government. He remained a Christian, however, and eventually wrote tracts and letters attacking Islam. In *Sources of Knowledge* John of Damascus wrote that Islam was a variant form of Christianity closely related to the heretical doctrine Arianism.

The Byzantine Empire was more willing to accommodate the practice of Islam than was western Europe. As early as 717, mosques were built within the walls of Constantinople for use by Muslim visitors to the imperial capital. Later, the Byzantine Empire would permit Muslim settlements within its territories; the Muslims were encouraged to convert to Christianity, but were not forced to do so.

Attacks on Islamic doctrine could not stop the growth of the Islamic state. During the ninth century Arab armies conquered Crete and Sicily, and even sacked Rome in 846; the Arabs established colonies along the Mediterranean coast of modern-day Italy. By the end of the century, the Abbasid caliphs ruled an area greater than that encompassed by the Roman Empire at its height.

But the unity of the Muslims under a single caliph did not last. As the empire grew, it required a large and complex bureaucracy to govern all of its outlying territories. Through the decentralization of the empire, the caliphs became figureheads who symbolized the unity of Muslims, rather than true spiritual and political leaders. And like the Umayyad caliphs, the Abbasids had proven more interested in acquiring the trappings of worldly power than in spreading Islam. "The caliph no longer regarded himself as the

. . . *imam* who led by personal example the faithful along the right-eous path," writes Caesar E. Farah in *Islam*. "He was now an absolute sovereign served by all the prerogatives due the despot; unlimited powers were at his disposal; he was beyond reach of the public, and fully capable of exercising such powers at will."

In some parts of the empire, groups of believers who felt that their interpretation of Islam was the correct one broke away from Abbasid rule completely. For example, in 969 the Fatimids, a group of Shiite Muslims, established an independent state in Egypt. Other independent kingdoms emerged in Persia, in northern India, and on the Anatolian Peninsula (modern-day Turkey). One group in particular, a Central Asian group of Sunni Muslims called the Seljuk Turks, became so powerful that in 1050 the caliph was forced to recognize the Seljuk sultan as "king of the East."

HOLY WARS

Christians fought back against the spread of Islam. Charles Martel and the Franks stopped the advance of the Moors into western Europe at the Battle of Poitiers (or Tours) in October 732. Gradually, the Christians began a counterattack. Muslim territory on the Iberian Peninsula was slowly recaptured by Christian armies in a series of wars, known as the *Reconquista* (Spanish for "Reconquest"), that lasted nearly 500 years. When the Reconquista was complete and the kingdom of Spain established in 1492, one of the first acts of the rulers Ferdinand and Isabella was to force all Muslims and Jews to convert to Christianity or be expelled from the country.

The early successes of the Reconquista would contribute to another series of Christian assaults on an area closer to the center of the Islamic world. In 1091 the Byzantine emperor asked Rome for assistance against the Turks. Pope Urban II responded in 1095 by calling for a campaign to buttress the Byzantine Empire and to recapture Jerusalem and the areas in which Jesus Christ and the apostles had performed their ministry. The pope promised that

The city of Acre is surrendered to crusaders during the Third Crusade. The Crusades were a series of wars fought over Jerusalem and the "Holy Land" from 1096 to 1291.

anyone who fell in battle against the Muslims would be forgiven of all sins and go straight to heaven.

Tens of thousands of Europeans set out on the First Crusade in two waves during 1096. The first group of crusaders was badly organized and undisciplined. On their way through central Europe these crusaders massacred entire Jewish communities. These crusaders were not well armed, either, and when they finally reached Asia Minor, the Turks slaughtered them. A second, better-prepared group of crusaders set out in the fall of 1096, and they were more successful. In July 1099, after a protracted siege, they captured Jerusalem. The victorious crusaders then slaughtered nearly all of the Muslims and Jews living in the city. Territory that the crusaders had captured in Palestine and Syria was broken into four Christian kingdoms, known as the Crusader States: Edessa, Antioch, Jerusalem, and Tripoli.

The Crusader States developed complex relationships with the Muslims that surrounded them. To protect their borders, the Christians frequently raided and skirmished with the Muslims, and they sometimes mistreated Muslims living within their kingdoms. Nonetheless, the Christians also traded with Muslims and intermarried with them.

Over the years Muslims counterattacked to gain back the lost territory. By 1187 Muslim forces under the Kurdish general Salah al-Din (better known in the West as Saladin) had recaptured Jerusalem and other important cities. In response, new Crusades were launched, leading to another century of warfare. In 1291 the Mamluks, who controlled a powerful empire in Egypt, launched a final offensive that destroyed the Crusader States.

This aerial view shows the remains of a crusader sea castle in modern-day Lebanon. In 1291 the Mamluks mounted an offensive that destroyed the Latin Crusader States on the eastern Mediterranean coast.

The Crusades did not really have much impact on Islam. The area over which Muslims and Christians were fighting was only a small part of the Islamic world, and the crusaders never truly threatened the control of the caliphs. Throughout the 13th century two other foes posed a greater threat to the Arab Islamic state: the Mamluks in Egypt and the Mongols of Asia. However, the Crusades shocked and humiliated many Muslims, just as the ultimate destruction of the Crusader States surprised and angered western Christians. Even today, this armed conflict between Christianity and Islam continues to tinge the relationship of these religions.

CULTURAL EXCHANGE AND COLONIALISM

The Crusades and the Spanish Reconquista would have a permanent influence on the culture of the Christian West. The crusaders were introduced to goods from Asia that were not available in Europe, such as spices and silks. Demand for these items would lead European countries to seek trade routes east and west. In addition, the learning of Europe was supplemented greatly by the scholarship of Muslims. In al-Andalus, ancient Greek and Roman texts had been preserved, and Muslim and Jewish scholars had written works that complemented and advanced these great works of philosophy and science. After Christians conquered Muslim cities like Toledo and Seville during the 13th century, scholars translated the ancient texts from Arabic into Latin and reintroduced them to the West. Europeans could then build on this knowledge, which might otherwise have been lost. As a result, Muslim scholarship made an important contribution to the European Renaissance, which began in Italy during the 14th century.

However, although Renaissance advances in science and technology had often been built on the discoveries of Muslim thinkers, Muslims rarely adapted new European ideas or technology for their own purposes. For centuries Muslims in Asia and Africa had considered Europeans to be crude and barbaric. This would place the Muslim world at a disadvantage as European states began to build worldwide colonial empires based on trade.

Portugal had been one of the first nations to send voyages of exploration and conquest. The Portuguese had learned shipbuild-

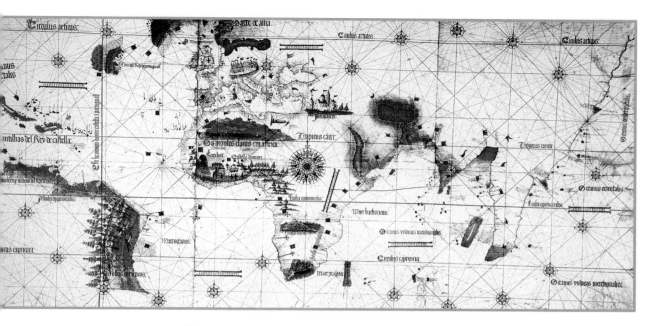

This Portuguese map from 1501 shows the lands "discovered" by European explorers, including the eastern coasts of North and South America (Brazil). The blue vertical line drawn through the Atlantic Ocean indicates the distribution of territory by Pope Alexander VI in 1494. New lands discovered east of that line were to be controlled by Portugal, and lands to the west by Spain. Soon, other European powers became involved in exploring and colonizing unknown lands, and by the end of the 18th century Great Britain, France, the Netherlands, and Spain possessed vast overseas empires.

ing and sail-making techniques from the Muslims of al-Andalus. In the early 15th century, Portuguese sailors ventured into the unknown Atlantic Ocean and south along the coast of Africa. One purpose of these voyages was to circle around Muslim territory. The Ottoman Turks blocked the land routes to the East, making goods from China and India very expensive in Europe. The Portuguese hoped to bypass the Ottomans by using sea routes to Asia. Gradually, Portuguese explorers worked their way along the west coast of Africa, establishing trading posts. The Portuguese rounded the continent's southernmost point in 1487, and 10 years later sent an expedition under Vasco da Gama that reached India.

When the Portuguese arrived in the Indian Ocean, they had a weapon that the Muslim inhabitants did not: the cannon. This enabled tiny Portugal to capture African, Arab, Persian, and Indian ports and dominate trade in the Indian Ocean.

Portuguese control over the trade routes with the East made the small country tremendously wealthy. It also encouraged other European nations to establish their own power over Islamic lands. By the 18th century the British had a great deal of influence in India, Persia, and coastal areas of the Arabian Peninsula; the Dutch ruled the Spice Islands (modern-day Indonesia); and Spain controlled the Philippines. The French invaded Egypt in 1798 and annexed Algeria in 1830.

As European powers grew stronger, the Islamic world fell into a period of decline. In 1683 the Ottoman Empire expanded west into Europe and threatened to capture Vienna, but after this high point the Ottomans gradually lost control of their eastern European territories in wars with Russia and Austria. Ottoman power and influence continued to wane as the European countries slowly picked the empire apart. By the end of the 19th century the once-glorious empire was being ridiculed throughout the West as "the sick man of Europe." At the end of World War I the empire was dissolved and its remaining territories in the Arab world were placed under European control.

Colonialism had a devastating effect on Muslim culture. The European powers took resources from the lands they ruled, which enabled them to maintain the strength of their empires. And Westerners imposed their religious, social, and political practices on the lands they colonized—frequently arguing that in so doing they were improving the lives of their "backward" colonial subjects. Traditional Muslim economic systems were torn apart and rebuilt according to Western norms. Independent artisans and merchants were replaced by factories that provided cheap labor and goods for their colonial masters. Schoolteachers were compelled to teach Western ideas and beliefs and to ignore their native traditions. People who wore traditional clothing rather than Western fashions were ridiculed. Although the colonial subjects were permitted to practice their traditional religions, colonial governments openly supported Christian missionaries who aggressively sought converts. These policies caused much resentment and anger among Muslims.

Muslims developed a number of political and social responses to Western expansion and to the decline of their civilization. Some Islamic reformers argued that Muslims should not simply accept or reject Western ideals, but should reinterpret traditional Islamic institutions and law in order to adapt to the contemporary situation. Others argued that the only path to survival and prosperity in the modern era was to adopt secular, Western-style modes of government and public life. A third group called for a return to the roots of the Islamic faith. Muslim societies had declined because the people had strayed from the true path of Islam, they claimed. The only way to revitalize Muslim societies was to reestablish religious legal authority over every sphere of life, these Muslims asserted. Today that point of view, espoused by Muslims often referred to as Islamic fundamentalists or Islamists, remains influential.

Nationalist movements—the desire by people to have their own state—had existed within the Ottoman Empire during the 19th century. When the empire was broken up during the 1920s, many new states were created, although these were placed under European control. After the end of World War II, however, the United States encouraged Great Britain, France, and other European powers to give up their colonial possessions. As a result, many countries in the Islamic world gained their freedom during the 1940s, 1950s, and 1960s.

RELATIONS BETWEEN MUSLIMS AND CHRISTIANS TODAY

Despite the history of violent and oppressive relations between Christianity and Islam, the two religions share many of the same values. Unfortunately, many Christians do not fully understand Islam, and many Muslims do not understand Christianity. For example, some evangelical Christians disagree that Allah is the same God they worship. Many of these people publicly displayed their outrage when President George W. Bush said at a November 2003 press conference that Christians and Muslims worship the same God. At the same time, some Muslims believe that Christianity is really a polytheistic religion because of its doctrine

The Dome of the Rock, a Muslim shrine, rises over the western wall of the ancient Temple in Jerusalem, a place sacred to Jews. Nearby is the Church of the Holy Sepulchre, which marks what Christians believe is the place where Jesus was crucified and buried. Because of Jerusalem's importance to each of the three monotheistic religions, Muslims, Christians, and Jews have often fought over control of the city.

of the Trinity as well as the Catholic Church's reverence for Mary, Jesus' mother.

In the United States, where the number of Muslims is growing, some people are making an effort to overcome the historical and cultural differences and learn more about each other. This became especially important in the aftermath of the September 11, 2001, terrorist attacks on the World Trade Center and Pentagon. As many people pointed out, it is important to remember that the attacks were politically motivated, and that although radical Muslims were involved, most Muslims condemned the attacks. Likewise, the subsequent U.S. invasions of Afghanistan and Iraq were undertaken for political purposes, rather than as a new crusade to oppress Muslims. Unfortunately, both Muslims and Christians often judge each other by the words and actions of religious extremists.

During his 2001 visit to Syria, Pope John Paul II spoke about the importance of Muslims and Christians learning how to live and work together:

> Interreligious dialogue is most effective when it springs from the experience of "living with each other" from day to day within the same community and culture. In Syria, Christians and Muslims have lived side by side for centuries, and a rich dialogue of life has gone on unceasingly. Every individual and every family knows moments of harmony and other moments when dialogue has broken down. The positive experiences must strengthen our communities in the hope of peace; and the negative experiences should not be allowed to undermine that hope. For all the times that Muslims and Christians have offended one another, we need to seek forgiveness from the Almighty and offer each other forgiveness. Jesus teaches us that we must pardon others' offenses if God is to pardon us our sins.

> As members of the one human family and as believers, we have obligations to the common good, to justice and to solidarity. Interreligious dialogue will lead to many forms of cooperation, especially in responding to the duty to care for the poor and weak. These are the signs that our worship of God is genuine.

Chronology

ca. 2000 B.C.E.   According to Jewish and Christian religious traditions, God establishes covenant with Abraham.

ca. 1500 B.C.E.   Moses is believed to have received the 10 Commandments on Mount Sinai.

ca. 961 B.C.E.   David, the greatest king of Israel, dies.

922 B.C.E. After the death of Solomon, during whose rule the Holy Temple was built in Jerusalem, Israel is divided into northern and southern kingdoms.

722 B.C.E. The Northern Kingdom (Israel) is destroyed by the Assyrians; its people, taken in captivity, become known as the "ten lost tribes."

586 B.C.E. Jerusalem falls to Babylon, and the Jews are taken into exile.

539 B.C.E. The Persians conquer Babylon, and Cyrus the Great allows Jews to return and rebuild their Temple.

516 B.C.E.   Reconstruction of the Temple is completed.

458 B.C.E. Ezra teaches the Jews how to understand God's law.

332 B.C.E. Alexander the Great conquers the Jewish territories in the Persian Empire.

198 B.C.E.   The Seleucids take control of Judea from the Ptolemies.

168 B.C.E.   Jews revolt against Antiochus IV Epiphanes, eventually gaining their freedom after four years of fighting.

63 B.C.E. Judea becomes a Roman province.

ca. 4 B.C.E. Jesus is born in Bethlehem.

ca. 29 C.E. Jesus is crucified and, his followers believe, rises from the dead.

46   Paul begins his first missionary journey.

70   The Temple in Jerusalem is destroyed in retaliation for a Jewish revolt

Chronology

against Roman authority.

161 Marcus Aurelius becomes emperor of Rome; under his rule Judaism and Christianity are outlawed.

ca. 200 The Mishnah is created by Judah the Prince.

312 Constantine attributes victory in an important battle to intervention by Jesus; the next year, as western Roman emperor, he issues the Edict of Milan, which declares religious toleration in the empire.

325 The Council of Nicaea is held.

391 Christianity becomes the official religion of the Roman Empire.

395 The Roman Empire is permanently divided into eastern and western halves.

476 Collapse of the western empire.

c. 570 Muhammad is born on the Arabian Peninsula.

622 The Muslims leave Mecca for Yathrib, where they establish the first Muslim community.

632 Muhammad dies.

661 The fourth caliph, Ali, is murdered; this event eventually leads Islam to become divided between Sunni and Shiite Muslims.

711 Muslim Moors from North Africa invade the Iberian Peninsula.

732 The Muslim advance into western Europe is halted at the Battle of Poitiers.

750 The Abbasid caliphs take control of the Islamic state.

912 Compilation of authoritative collections of Hadith is completed.

1054 The Great Schism permanently divides the Roman Catholic and Greek Orthodox churches.

Chronology

1095 Pope Urban II preaches the First Crusade in Claremont, France.

1099 European Christian knights of the First Crusade capture Jerusalem, massacre Jewish and Muslim inhabitants.

1453 The Ottoman Turks capture Constantinople and put an end to the Byzantine Empire.

1492 The Spanish Reconquista is completed as the Muslims are expelled from their last stronghold on the Iberian Peninsula.

1517 Martin Luther posts his "95 Theses," questioning certain Roman Catholic practices; this sets in motion events that ultimately lead to the Protestant Reformation.

1919 Following World War I, the defeated Ottoman Empire loses its remaining territories in the Middle East; France and Great Britain eventually receive mandates from the League of Nations to administer Arab lands formerly under Ottoman control.

1920s Zionism—the movement to establish a Jewish homeland in Palestine—gains momentum; the arrival of thousands of Jewish settlers causes friction with Palestinian Arabs, and Jewish-Arab violence continues throughout the 1930s.

1939–45 As World War II is fought, Nazi Germany attempts to exterminate all European Jews, ultimately killing an estimated 6 million.

1947 The United Nations adopts a plan to partition Palestine into two states, one Jewish and the other Palestinian Arab.

1948 The state of Israel is proclaimed in May, and Arab nations immediately attack; by the time all fighting ceases early the following year, Israel has won territorial gains, and the Palestinians are left without a homeland.

Chronology

1965 During the Second Vatican Council, the Roman Catholic Church officially repudiates the idea that Jews are guilty of deicide for the crucifixion of Jesus.

1967 Israel wins swift, decisive victory over Egypt, Syria, and Jordan in the Six-Day War; takes control of East Jerusalem, the West Bank, and the Gaza Strip, bringing hundreds of thousands of Palestinians under its military occupation.

1987 The first Palestinian *intifada*, or uprising against Israeli rule, breaks out in the occupied West Bank and Gaza Strip.

1993 The Oslo Accords between Israel and the Palestinians establish a framework for peace, including the possibility of an independent Palestinian Arab state.

2000 The second Palestinian *intifada* breaks out, derailing the peace process and inaugurating an extended cycle of violence and retaliation in Israel and the occupied territories.

2001 Terrorists from the Muslim extremist organization al-Qaeda fly commercial jets into the World Trade Center in New York City and the Pentagon, near Washington, D.C.; United States and allies invade Afghanistan, whose fundamentalist Muslim government, the Taliban, harbors al-Qaeda leaders; Taliban government is quickly toppled.

2003 The United States invades Iraq, topples regime of Saddam Hussein; U.S. president George W. Bush frames invasion as part of U.S. "war on terrorism."

2005 Despite unrest, Iraq holds elections to establish a national government.

Glossary

animism—a primitive religion in which all things in nature are believed to have conscious spirits, and a supernatural force is believed to animate the universe.

apologist—a person who speaks or writes in defense of an idea or individual.

covenant—a solemn and binding agreement between two parties; a compact.

deicide—the act of killing God, or someone who commits that act.

dogma—a belief or a set of beliefs that a religion holds to be true.

ecumenical—representing the whole of a body of churches.

Gentile—anyone who is not of the Jewish faith.

henotheist—one who worships a single God but does not deny the possible existence of other gods.

monotheist—one who believes in the existence of a single, all-powerful God.

pogrom—an organized massacre of Jews.

polytheistic—relating to belief in, or worship of, multiple gods.

proselytize—to try to win converts to one's religious faith.

scripture—a body of writings considered sacred or authoritative by adherents of a particular religion.

theology—the study of religious faith, practice, and experience, especially the study of God and God's relationship to the universe.

umma—the worldwide community of Muslims.

Further Reading

Armstrong, Karen. *Islam: A Short History.* New York: Random House, 2000.

Farah, Caesar E. *Islam.* 7th ed. New York: Barron's Educational Series, 2003.

Halverson, Dean, general editor. *The Illustrated Guide to World Religions.* Bloomington, Minn.: Bethany House Publishers, 2003.

Johnson, Paul. *A History of Christianity.* New York: Atheneum, 1976.

Lewis, Bernard, ed. *The World of Islam: Faith, People, Culture.* New York: Thames and Hudson, 2002.

Olson, Roger E. *The Story of Christian Theology: Twenty Centuries of Tradition and Reform.* Downers Grove, Ill.: InterVarsity Press, 1999.

Pfeiffer, Charles E. *Old Testament History.* Washington, D.C.: Canon Press, 1973.

Robinson, George. *Essential Judaism: A Complete Guide to Beliefs, Customs, and Rituals.* New York: Simon and Schuster, 2000.

Internet Resources

http://www.arches.uga.edu/~godlas/islamwest.html

This comprehensive page includes essays and links to online sources on Islamic history, culture, sects, law, scripture, and contemporary issues.

http://www.islamamerica.org/index.cfm

The website of Dar al Islam, a non-profit organization that promotes understanding between Muslims and non-Muslims in the United States, includes recent articles on politics, culture, and history.

http://www.newadvent.org/cathen/

The Catholic Encyclopedia, which was originally published early in the 20th century, is a searchable database of articles about important people and events in the history of Christianity.

http://www.rationalchristianity.net

This webpage provides basic information about Christianity, and answers some of the most common questions about the religion.

http://www.jewfaq.org

The website Judaism 101 provides information about Jewish beliefs, history, customs, holidays, practices, and scriptures.

Index

Numbers in **bold italic** refer to captions.

Index

Index

Picture Credits

Contributors

General Editor DR. SHAMS INATI is Professor of Islamic Studies at Villanova University and was a Fulbright scholar at Balamand University during the editing process of this work. She is a specialist in Islamic philosophy and theology and has published widely in the field. Her publications include *Remarks and Admonitions, Part One: Logic* (1984), *Our Philosophy* (1987), *Ibn Sina and Mysticism* (1996), *The Second Republic of Lebanon* (1999), *The Problem of Evil: Ibn Sina's Theodicy* (2000), and *Iraq: Its History, People, and Politics* (2003). She has also written a large number of articles that have appeared in books, journals, and encyclopedias.

   Dr. Inati has been the recipient of a number of awards and honors, including an Andrew Mellon Fellowship, an Endowment for the Humanities grant, a U.S. Department of Defense grant, and a Fulbright grant. For further information about her work, see www.homepage.villanova.edu/shams.inati.

DOROTHY KAVANAUGH is a freelance writer who lives near Philadelphia. She is a graduate of Bryn Mawr College and the mother of four children. This is her first book.